MW01277607

ISBN: 9781290813242

Published by:
HardPress Publishing
8345 NW 66TH ST #2561
MIAMI FL 33166-2626

Email: info@hardpress.net
Web: http://www.hardpress.net

THE ROYAL BANK
OF CANADA

The Royal Bank of Canada
Head Office Building
Montreal

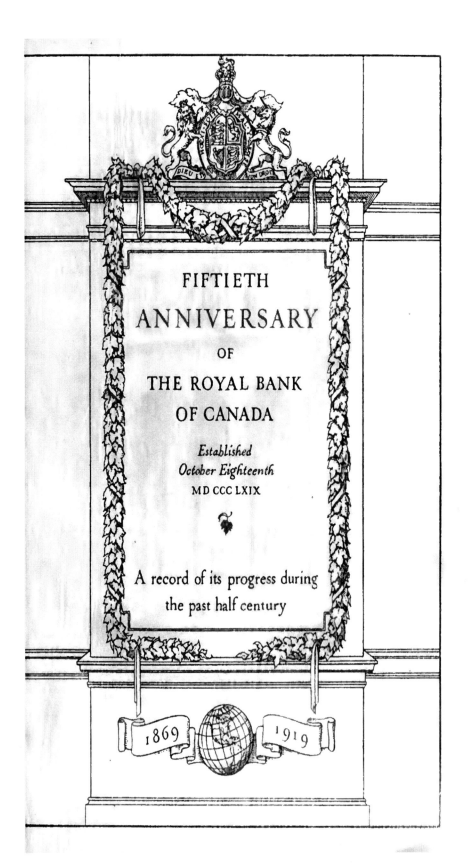

FIFTIETH
ANNIVERSARY
OF
THE ROYAL BANK
OF CANADA

Established
October Eighteenth
MD CCC LXIX

A record of its progress during
the past half century

1869   1919

The Royal Bank of Canada
and Office Building
Montreal

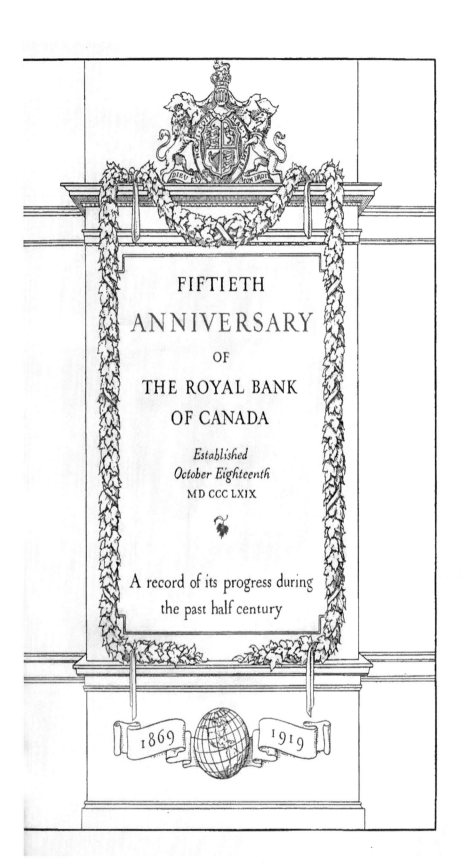

FIFTIETH
ANNIVERSARY
OF
THE ROYAL BANK
OF CANADA

Established
October Eighteenth
MD CCC LXIX

A record of its progress during
the past half century

1869   1919

CONTENTS

DESIGNED, ENGRAVED AND PRINTED BY
THE RONALDS PRESS
AND ADVERTISING AGENCY LIMITED
MONTREAL, QUE.

INTRODUCTION

TO COMMEMORATE *its found-ation fifty years ago The Royal Bank of Canada sends forth this book. Here are described its modest beginning, the development of its expansive policy, and its phenomenal growth. The history is supplemented by a chronology of events, a summary of the bank's position at the end of each year, and an Honour Roll of all the members of the staff who enlisted for active service in the Great War. The volume is presented as a record of past achievement and a source of inspiration for the future.*

T. E. Kenny
President 1870-1908

T. E. Kenny
President 1870-1908

THE ROYAL BANK OF CANADA

A Summary of its History
from the year 1869 to the present date

THE Golden Jubilee, which The Royal Bank of Canada now celebrates, is but a milestone in the onward march of an institution which has developed with the Dominion, and stretched far beyond its bounds.

The bank had its origin in stirring times. Civil War in the United States was at its height. The North offered an eager market for all kinds of produce, while blockade-runners carrying on trade with the Southern Confederacy swarmed in the port of Halifax. Profits were phenomenal and the city was in its heyday of prosperity. The air was full of constructive schemes, and in order to increase trading facilities Messrs. T. C. Kinnear and John Duffus retired from the directorate of the Union Bank of Halifax to join a number of other influential citizens in a financial co-partnership under the name of the Merchants Bank. The objects and purposes of the new enterprise, with the names of its founders, were set forth in the following advertisement in the Halifax Recorder:

"Halifax, 26th April, 1864

"The subscribers having entered into co-partnership, under the name and firm of the Merchants Bank, beg respectfully to announce that on and after Monday next, the 2nd of May, they will be prepared at their banking house in Bedford Row to discount promissory notes and acceptances, make advances on approved securities, purchase and sell bills of exchange, receive money on deposit, and transact all other business matters connected with a *business* establishment.

J. W. MERKEL, *President*	WILLIAM CUNARD
EDWARD KENNY	JOHN TOBIN
T. C. KINNEAR	GEORGE P. MITCHELL
JOHN DUFFUS	JEREMIAH NORTHUP

"N.B. Banking hours from 10 to 3.
"The Board will meet for discount daily (Sundays excepted).

J. W. MERKEL, *President*
GEORGE MACLEAN, *Cashier*"

The firm met with immediate success, and during the first five years of its operation earnings averaged nine per cent. per annum. At this time a change in the form of organization became obligatory. Confederation of the provinces, under the British North America Act of 1867, gave to the new Parliament of Canada exclusive jurisdiction in all matters pertaining to banks and banking, and it was foreseen that the Dominion Bank Act then under discussion would no longer permit the enjoyment of full banking privileges by co-partnership associations. It therefore became necessary to apply for a Federal charter, and an Act incorporating the Merchants Bank of Halifax received Royal assent on June 22nd, 1869. The authorized capital was $1,000,000, of which at first, only $500,000 was offered for subscription.

Such was the confidence inspired by the administration of the old co-partnership that more than one hundred prominent Nova Scotians availed themselves of the opportunity to become associated with the re-organization. On October 18th, 1869, the first general meeting of shareholders was held, and Messrs. William Cunard, J. B. Duffus, T. C. Kinnear, Thomas E. Kenny, John

Taylor, M. Dwyer and Edward Smith were elected directors. A statement of the business of the late proprietary institution up to October 1st was read, which showed a paid-up capital of $300,000, a Reserve Fund of $20,000, Deposits of $284,656, Current Loans of $266,970, and Total Assets of $729,163. At the first meeting of directors on the following day Thomas C. Kinnear was unanimously chosen President.

Times had changed since 1864. With the surrender of the South, war-time prosperity had ended; the failure of the fisheries in '67 and '68 had caused great distress in the coastal villages of Nova Scotia; and the expiry of the Reciprocity Treaty with the United States had deprived Halifax of a paying trade in many commodities. It was a time for caution, and one of the by-laws of the bank, afterwards repealed, provided that no discounts what- ever should be granted unless approved by the President and at least one Director. Business increased so rapidly that President Kinnear soon found himself unable to devote the necessary time to the duties of his office, and Thomas E. Kenny, son of one of the original founders, who had already given proof of outstanding ability, was elected his successor.

The former co-partnership had been local in its operations, but the new President had a vision of an expanding bank, and branches were opened at Pictou in 1870, at Antigonish, Bridge-water, Lunenburg, Truro and Weymouth in 1871, and at Sydney in 1872. So prudent was the administration of Mr. Kenny and his co-directors that at the fourth annual meeting he was able to make the announcement, unique in banking annals, that during the year 1872, with current loans amounting to $1,278,850, the bank had not lost one dollar by bad debts. A dividend of eight per cent. was declared and $40,000 added to the Reserve.

The year 1873 was an anxious one in Nova Scotia. The suspension in the month of April of the Bank of Acadia, followed by the closing of the doors of the Bank of Liverpool, caused the collapse of the business community in the section of the province in which they had operated. While the Merchants Bank of Halifax suffered some loss through customers involved in these failures, the President in his next annual report was able to announce the usual dividend and a further addition of $40,000 to the Reserve. This fund was augmented by $50,000 and $30,000 respectively in 1874 and 1875 despite the universal trade depression which had followed the great financial panic in the United States.

During the first six years of its existence, three of which had tested the strength of older institutions, the bank had increased its paid-up capital from $300,000 to $900,000; its Reserve Fund from $20,000 to $180,000; and its Assets from $714,948 to $2,594,917. It had also extended its business to the neighbouring province of Prince Edward Island by the establishment of branches at Charlottetown in 1873 and at Summerside in 1874.

Hard times continued, not only in Canada but throughout the world, accentuated in Nova Scotia by a decline in wooden shipbuilding, which had long been the mainstay and chief industry of the province. Restricted circulation and the necessary contraction of loans and discounts lessened the profits of all banks; many reduced their capital and three failed. The utmost the Merchants Bank of Halifax could hope to do until the return of more prosperous conditions, was to retain the ground already gained, and to strengthen its organization.

Up to this time branches had been in charge of local men, often interested in other pursuits and not seldom politicians,

Sir Herbert Holt, K.B.
Vice-President 1907
President since 1908

Sir Herbert Holt, K.B.
Vice-President 1907
President since 1908

two becoming members of the Legislature. While they had rendered able service to the bank, it was felt that branch management in future should be entrusted to trained officials, and a policy was adopted that henceforth, as opportunity offered and vacancies occurred, only men who could give undivided attention to banking should be appointed local agents.

As the premises at Halifax had long been inadequate for the growing needs of the bank, it was resolved in 1876 to erect a structure suited to its requirements. One of the best sites in the city was secured and the building was ready for occupancy in May 1879. On March 3rd, 1880, the President stated "Our institution, in common with others, has carried its full share of the burden imposed by the dull times. It is now in a position to take advantage of any improvement in business when it arises." On this occasion Mr. Kenny also claimed with some pride that notwithstanding the long-continued commercial stagnation, the bank had always made a fair profit and had paid $500,000 in dividends to the shareholders since its organization. At this meeting Mr. Michael Dwyer was elected to succeed Senator Northup, who had passed away in the previous April. Senator Northup had been the first Vice-President, and his excellent judgment combined with his intimate knowledge of the affairs of the province had contributed in no small degree to the steady progress of the bank.

By 1882 conditions in Nova Scotia had begun to improve, and the bank entered upon a period of renewed branch extension, chiefly in New Brunswick. But a more ambitious scheme was maturing in the minds of the directorate. The trade of Halifax was largely sea-borne and its merchants had long carried on a profitable exchange of commodities with its natural markets, the Bermudas, the Bahamas and the West Indies. In the hope of creating a new field of business enterprise for the bank a step was taken which is thus recorded in the minutes:

"*30th March, 1882*

"Mr. Duncan, the Accountant, having been confined in his house through a severe attack of rheumatism, the President being of opinion that his (Mr. D's) health was not fully re-established, suggested a visit to Bermuda, to which the Board assented. Mr. Duncan was accordingly advised by his physicians to avail himself of this opportunity, as calculated to do him much good, and he was also authorized by the Board in the event of his finding a suitable opening to establish an agency of the bank at Hamilton."

Mr. Duncan upon his return reported that after considerable difficulty, and with misgivings as to its success, he had completed arrangements for an agency in Hamilton. This branch, after languishing for some years, was closed, as well as one established later at St. Pierre Miquelon. These seeming failures, however, were but stepping stones to future success, for the experience gained proved invaluable when the bank again entered the foreign field.

Towards the close of 1882 Mr. Duncan was appointed Cashier, and on January 18th following, Edson L. Pease, who was the instrument of a great expansive movement in a later decade, became the Accountant at the Halifax office—after a period of eight years' service with the Canadian Bank of Commerce. In this year (1883) the paid-up capital stock was increased to $1,000,000 and $20,000 was added to the Reserve. Normal trade conditions had not yet been restored and many Maritime Province banks were finding it difficult to recover from the effect of past depression. On June 14th the Directors had declined to purchase the Merchants Bank of Prince Edward Island, which offered to sell out its interests. A little later a similar proposition was received from the Mari-

[16]

time Bank of Canada, which had its headquarters at St. John, New Brunswick. This institution had suffered severe losses and after an investigation of its affairs, conducted by Mr. Pease, the Board of the Merchants Bank decided not to recommend amalgamation to its shareholders. Four years later the Maritime Bank suspended payment, and only $10\frac{6}{10}$ cents on the dollar was received by its depositors.

The Merchants Bank of Halifax was not destined to pass through these trying times unscathed and in 1885 it suffered one of those heavy losses which occasionally all banks have to face. Two of Nova Scotia's greatest industries, largely indebted to the bank, passed into the hands of receivers. The profits of the year were wiped out and the Rest drawn upon for $80,000. The trouble was taken at the roots and within three years the loss had been more than made good and the Reserve Fund restored to its former strength. Moreover, it was now realized that if enterprises of national importance were to be financed, the bank must become national in its scope—with capital and reserves so large that its position could not be shaken by local losses.

It was therefore resolved in 1887 to extend operations to the City of Montreal and to appoint Edson L. Pease manager of the new branch. To build up a business in a centre which was the headquarters of so many powerful banking organizations was no light undertaking, but progress was steady. Soon the first premises became inadequate; more desirable quarters were secured, and with the opening of agencies in the city—east and west—the Merchants Bank of Halifax became firmly established in the metropolis of the Dominion.

This had been accomplished during a period when the development of Canada was retarded by world events. The failure of

Baring Bros. in 1890, through default of the Argentine Government in payment of its obligations, created a suspicion in England as to the soundness of all foreign investments and temporarily checked the flow of capital to the Dominion; while the passage of the McKinley Tariff Bill lessened exports to the United States. Three years later occurred the worst panic in the history of the Republic, following President Cleveland's Venezuelan Message, and this crisis had its reflex in Canada, causing great depreciation in the market price of securities.

Through all this financial disquietude, and notwithstanding the low rates obtainable for call money—sometimes one-fourth of one per cent. in England and one per cent. in New York—the Merchants Bank of Halifax continued to strengthen its position. It added year by year to its Reserves and in 1895, to meet the requirements of its growing business, increased the paid-up capital stock to $1,500,000.

At this time (1895) Newfoundland suffered its second great disaster. The fire which had devastated its capital city in 1892 was now followed by failure of all its banks, and a branch was opened in St. John's to assist in the restoration of banking accommodation in the stricken Colony.

In 1898 Mr. Duncan ceased his exclusive management of the institution, although he remained for one year longer in charge of the head office in Halifax and of the branches in the Maritime Provinces and Newfoundland. During the fifteen years of his administration deposits had quadrupled; the reserve fund had been increased by nearly $1,000,000 and the total assets by more than $7,000,000.

With the commencement of an era of business prosperity throughout the Dominion in 1897, renewed expansion, under the direction of Mr. Pease, was determined upon. Branches were opened in the British Columbian mining towns of Nelson and Rossland and at the port of Vancouver, and in the following year in Grand Forks, Nanaimo and Victoria. No sooner had this leap been made to the Pacific coast than advantage was taken of an opportunity which had arisen in another direction.

The close of the Spanish-American war found the island of Cuba—a land of latent possibilities with inadequate banking facilities—about to enjoy a stable government after a long period of civil disturbances. The time seemed favorable for the introduction of modern banking methods, and Mr. Pease visited Havana in November, 1898, to enquire into the advisability of opening a branch in that city. So greatly was he impressed with the future prospects of the island that he recommended the Board of Directors to enter the new field without delay. The Peace of Paris, by which Cuba was granted independence, was signed on December 10th, 1898, and a month later, before ratification of the treaty, a branch of the bank was established under the management of W. F. Brock and of the former acting United States Consul and Consul-General for Cuba, J. A. Springer. After a year's service in Cuba Mr. Brock returned to Canada and F. J. Sherman and O. A. Hornsby, the latter now President of the Trust Company of Cuba, were appointed to act with Mr. Springer as Joint Managers. The bank soon gained the confidence of the public and the success of the Havana branch was the forerunner of a movement which already has encircled the Caribbean and stretched far down the eastern coast of South America.

As much of the Cuban trade had been diverted from Spain to the United States and exchange transactions with the Republic soon formed an important part of the business of the bank, this entry into the West Indies hastened a step which home needs had long rendered desirable, and an agency was established in the City of New York in May 1899. Later in the year a branch was also opened in Ottawa.

More money was required for all this expansion, and $500,000 of new stock was issued at 100 per cent. premium, and almost entirely paid up by the close of 1899. At the annual meeting of February 14th, 1900, a further issue of $1,000,000 was authorized.

At the same meeting another proposal of far-reaching importance was submitted to the shareholders. The bank had become an international institution and it was felt that a more comprehensive title should be adopted to accord with its position. A change of name to The Royal Bank of Canada was therefore recommended and approved. Parliamentary sanction was applied for and obtained and the new name came into operation on January 2nd, 1901.

In the following year, with the unanimous consent of the shareholders, a sale of 5000 shares of the capital stock of the bank at $250 per share was made to a number of prominent Americans among whom were the Blairs of New York, G. F. Baker, President of the First National Bank, New York, J. J. Mitchell, President of the Illinois Trust & Savings Bank, Chicago, Ogden Armour, Norman B. Ream, P. A. Valentine and Marshall Field, of Chicago. The purchase was made after a thorough examination of the affairs of the bank, and the connection thus established proved most beneficial to its interests.

The bank's growing business in Cuba was further extended by the purchase in 1903 of the assets of the Banco de Oriente in Santiago, and in 1904 of the Banco del Comercio, Havana, and its sphere of influence was widened when on September 14th of

Edson L. Pease
General Manager 1899
Vice-President since 1906 also
Managing Director since 1916

C. E. Neill
General Manager since 1916

entry into the West Indies hastened a step which home needs had long rendered desirable, and an agency was established in the City of New York in May 19.. Later in the year a branch was also opened in Ottawa.

More money was required for all this expansion, and $500,000 of new stock was issued ... one per cent. premium, and almost entirely paid up by the ... 1899. At the annual meeting of February 14th, 190. a further issue of $1,000,000 was authorized.

At the same time another proposal of far-reaching importance was ... consideration. The bank had become an international ... It was felt that a more comprehensive title should ... in accord with its position. A change of name ... Royal Bank of Canada was therefore recommended and ... necessary sanction was applied for and obtained ... came into operation on January 2nd, 190.

In the interest ... the unanimous consent of the shareholders, ... shares of the capital stock of the bank at $250 per share ... a number of prominent Americans among whom were ... of New York, G. F. Baker, President of the First National ... New York, J. J. Mitchell, President of the Illinois Trust & Savings Bank, Chicago, Ogden Armour, Norman B. Ream, ... and the late Marshall Field, of Chicago. The purchase ... examination of the affairs of the ... than established proved most ...

The bank ... was further extended by the purchase in 190. ... Banco de Oriente in Santiago, and in 1904 of the Banco ... merito, Havana, and its sphere of influence was widened ... ember 14th of

{ 20 }

Edson L. Pease
General Manager 1899
Vice-President since 1908, also
Managing Director since 1916

C. E. Neill
General Manager since 1916

the same year it was appointed Agent of the Government for the distribution throughout the Island of $31,000,000 awarded to the Army of Liberation, which constituted fifty per cent. of the amount of the soldiers' claims. So satisfactorily was this commission executed that in the following year the contract was extended to the distribution of the remainder of the award, $30,-000,000. As faith in its stability and conservative management became general, much of the wealth which had been hoarded during the years of political unrest was entrusted to the bank. Deposits steadily increased and branches were opened in Camaguey in 1904 and at Matanzas and Cardenas in 1905.

Meanwhile, with the commencement of a new century, the field at home had swiftly widened. There was great industrial activity and agricultural prosperity, and new settlements were springing up throughout the Canadian North-West. The bank prepared for another forward movement and at the annual meeting of February 14th, 1906, the shareholders approved the proposal of the Board to change the head office of the bank from Halifax to Montreal, the natural centre for expansion. Parliamentary sanction was obtained and on March 2nd, 1907, the head office was transferred. Additional directors were elected in harmony with the projected development and Thomas Ritchie, of Halifax, after serving many years as Vice-President, retired in favor of Herbert S. Holt, of Montreal. New stock of $900,000 was issued at $110 per cent. premium and $990,000 was added to the Reserve. During 1906 and the three succeeding years the bank more than doubled its branches; fifty were opened in Ontario and the North-West and five in Cuba, while the business in the West Indies was further extended to San Juan in Porto Rico, and Nassau in the Bahamas.

On October 26th, 1908, Mr. Thomas E. Kenny died at Hali-

fax, and the following tribute to his memory appeared in the
Annual Report of that year: "During the whole of his Presidency
of nearly forty years, Mr. Kenny devoted his rare and conspicuous
talents to the furtherance of the welfare of this bank. By his death
the bank has lost an able financier and a wise counsellor, and every
member of its staff a warm friend."

During his tenure of office the bank had grown from local
to international importance, with a paid-up capital of $3,900,000,
Reserve Fund of $4,600,000, total assets of $50,470,000, and
107 branches.

At a special meeting of Directors on November 16th, 1908,
Herbert S. Holt was elected President, and Edson L. Pease, already a Director, became Vice-President and also retained the
general management of the bank.

The accession of the new president marked the inaugur-
ation of a still broader policy, and the bank now effected a series
of four great mergers. By the purchase of the assets of the Union
Bank of Halifax in 1910 the whole territory of the Maritime
Provinces was covered and a branch in Port of Spain, Trinidad,
added to the West Indian service. This was followed in 1912 by
the absorption of the Traders Bank of Canada, which had one of
the best connections in Ontario, a province in which the Royal
Bank hitherto had not been largely represented. Four years later
the Quebec Bank was taken over. This historic institution had
weathered the financial storms of a century and its branches ma-
terially strengthened the Royal Bank in the Province of Quebec.
In 1918 the organization was balanced throughout the Dominion
by the acquisition of the Northern Crown Bank with a number
of well-located branches in Western Canada. There were now no
cities and but few towns in Canada in which the bank was not re-

presented. These mergers resulted also in the addition to the Board of men possessing an intimate knowledge of the needs and resources of the new territory, and E. F. B. Johnston, K.C., of Toronto, was elected 2nd Vice-President.

While these amalgamations were taking place the bank had acquired by purchase two important connections in foreign fields. It became established in the principal trading centre and port of Central America by taking over in 1912 the Bank of British Honduras at Belize, and a long desired entry was made into the only British possession on the southern continent by the acquisition in 1914 of the Bank of British Guiana. This step was taken not only on account of the growing trade with the Dominion but because of the undeveloped possibilities of the Colony.

The wave of prosperity in Canada had reached its crest in the year 1912. Too much of the money which had flowed into the country had been used in land speculation, unsound company promotion, and municipal extravagance, instead of in productive enterprise. The inevitable reaction from this reckless spending, which the banks had done all in their power to check, was followed by widespread business depression, increased by the sudden outbreak of war. The Minister of Finance, Sir Thomas White, promptly introduced emergency measures which controlled the situation. A general moratorium was averted and amidst almost universal financial upheaval Canada experienced no grave disturbance. The Directors, however, deemed it prudent to prepare for any contingency which might arise and in point of liquid assets the statement presented for the year 1914 was the strongest thus far submitted.

Under the exigencies of war Canada now sprang to the pinnacle of endeavor, and the resources of her financial institutions were taxed to the uttermost. The demand for foodstuffs about to arise in Europe was foreseen and the Royal, in common with other banks, encouraged the farmer to increase production. Acting under special legislation, advances were made for the first time on seed grain and to breeders of cattle. The bank also shared in proportion to its paid-up capital, in loans aggregating $345,000,000, to the Imperial and Dominion Governments for the purchase in Canada of munitions and other war materials and grain.

A marvellous industrial and agricultural expansion and the sale of commodities at record prices enabled the Dominion to make an astounding financial recovery and she was transformed from a debtor to a creditor nation. Advantage was taken of this great improvement in the monetary situation to float a series of internal loans, from the proceeds of which she not only provided for her own war needs but extended credit to the Allies. The bank supported these loans in every way and through its branches assisted in receiving and recording subscriptions, and in delivery of the bonds.

The tropical region of the West Indies and Central and South America found under war conditions an unlooked for and highly profitable opening for increased trade. With Germany blockaded, the field became the nearest available source of supply for sugar, and on the production of this staple all energies were concentrated. Other products sold at high prices and wealth accumulated. Keeping pace with this development, and the growing business with Canada under the Reciprocity Treaty of 1913, the Royal Bank rapidly extended its operations. Cuba was entirely covered with branches and a chain formed through the West Indies. Costa Rica was entered at San José (1915) and South America still further penetrated by the opening of branches in 1916 in Venezuela, with the approval and support of the British Government.

F. J. Sherman
Superior of Cuban Branches 1901-1911
Assistant General Manager since 1917

W. B. Torrance
Superintendent of Branches 1904-1911

were taxed to the uttermost. The demand for foodstuffs about to
arise in Europe was foreseen and the Royal, in common with
other banks, encouraged the farmer to increase production. Acting
under special legislation, advances were made for the first time on
seed grain and to breeders of cattle. The bank also shared in proportion to its paid-up capital, in loans aggregating $345,000,000,
to the Imperial and Dominion Governments for the purchase in
Canada of munitions and other war materials and grain.

A marvellous industrial and agricultural expansion and the
sale of commodities at record prices enabled the Dominion to
make an astounding financial recovery and she was transformed
from a debtor to a creditor nation. Advantage was taken of this
great improvement in the monetary situation to float a series of internal loans, from the proceeds of which she not only provided for
her own war needs but extended credit to the Allies. The bank supported these loans in every way and through its branches assisted in
receiving and recording subscriptions, and in delivery of the bonds.

The tropical region of the West Indies and Central and South
America found in war conditions an unlooked for and highly
profitable opening for increased trade. With Germany blockaded,
the field became the nearest available source of supply for sugar,
and on the production of this staple all energies were concentrated.
Other products sold at high prices and wealth accumulated.
Keeping pace with this development, and the growing business
with Canada under the Reciprocity Treaty of 1913, the Royal
Bank rapidly increased in operations. Cuba was entirely covered
with branches and a chain formed through the West Indies. Costa
Rica was entered at San José (1915) and South America still
further penetrated by the opening of branches in 1916 in Venezuela, with the approval and support of the British Government.

F. J. Sherman
Supervisor of Cuban Branches 1901-1911
Assistant General Manager since 1907

W. B. Torrance
Superintendent of Branches 1902-1917

Distinction had been reflected upon the bank in January, 1915, when the Order of Knighthood was conferred upon its President, Herbert S. Holt.

Early in the following year, at the annual general meeting, a new office was created and Edson L. Pease became Managing-Director, C. E. Neill succeeding him as General Manager.

The war period had been for the bank one of enormous growth. Its assets increased by more than $54,000,000 in 1916, by $82,000,000 in 1917, and by $92,000,000 in 1918. These results were attributed by Mr. Neill to four causes—"prosperous conditions in Canada and the West Indies, the advantageous location of branches, co-operation on the part of Directors, and a loyal and efficient staff."

Meanwhile the honor of the bank had been worthily upheld overseas. Where a whole nation responded so nobly, no special distinction can be claimed for the part in the conflict borne by one institution, but the long roll of 1,493 enlistments tells how eagerly the men of the Royal Bank answered the call to arms. The proudest page in its history is the record of those who for our security served so valiantly, and of the unreturning, who to service added sacrifice.

The branches already established in foreign fields had proved both advantageous to the bank and of the utmost importance from a national standpoint. Not only had improved facilities been afforded to Canadian exporters where they already had trade connections, but new ground had been broken for their enterprise. A further advance in this direction was made in 1918-19 by the opening of branches in Spain, at Barcelona; in France, at Paris; in Brazil, at Rio de Janeiro; in Argentine, at Buenos Aires; and in Uruguay, at Montevideo.

[29]

Reviewing the past success of the bank in this expansive policy at a meeting of shareholders held on January 9th, 1919, Mr. Pease made the following statement:—

"Our foreign deposits have always exceeded our foreign commercial loans, as the Government returns show. The present excess is over $15,000,000. We have now had twenty years' experience of banking in Cuba, the West Indies and Central America. During this period our losses have been infinitesimal—much under the percentage incurred in Canada, because the business represents chiefly the movement of staples, accommodation paper being inconsiderable. That Canada's trade is benefited by these branches is shown by the numerous business enquiries received. At the same time it cannot be said that we have neglected home interests. The number of our branches in Canada exceeds that of any other bank."

The efforts of the bank to extend its facilities abroad resulted in April, 1919, in a reciprocal working arrangement being entered into with one of England's greatest institutions, the London County Westminster & Parr's Bank, Ltd., with its network of more than 700 branches in the United Kingdom, France, Belgium and Spain. Through the purchase by this London bank of 10,000 shares of Royal Bank stock Canadian, American and British interests were linked and the bank became representative of a strong economic Anglo-Saxon union.

On November 30th, 1919, its fiftieth anniversary, The Royal Bank of Canada, with a paid-up capital stock of $17,000,000, reserve fund of $17,000,000, deposits of $419,121,000, loans of $284,083,000, total assets of $533,647,000, 622 branches, and a staff of 5,176, had gained a place in the list of the great banks of the world.

T.C. Kinnear
President 1869-1879

Thos Ritchie
Vice-President 1869-1879

Hon. J. Northup
Vice-President 1872-1879

Reviewing the p... ...cess of the bank in this expansive policy at a meeting of ... ...holders held on January 9th, 1919,. Mr. Pease made the ... ... statement:—

"Our foreign dep... have always exceeded our foreign commercial loan... ...overnment returns show. The present excess is over $1... ... We have now had twenty years' experience of banking ... Canada, the West Indies and Central America. During this ... ...r losses have been infinitesimal—much under the percent... ...curred in Canada, because the business represents chie... ...ement of staples, accommodation paper being increase ... that Canada's trade is benefited by these branches ... ... numerous business enquiries received. At the same ... ...cannot be said that we have neglected home interests. ... ... of our branches in Canada exceeds that of any other ...

The eff... ... the bank to extend its facilities abroad resulted in April ... ... a reciprocal working arrangement being entered into with one of England's greatest institutions, the London County Westminster & Parr's Bank, Ltd., with its network of more than ... ... branches in the United Kingdom, France, Belgium and Spain. Through the purchase by this London bank of 10,000 shares of Royal Bank stock Canadian, American and British interests were linked and the bank became representative of a strong economic Anglo-Saxon union.

On November 30th, 1919, its fiftieth anniversary, The Royal Bank of ... ... with a paid-up capital stock of $17,000,000, reserve fu... ... $17,000,000, deposits of $419,121,000, loans of $... ... total assets of $533,647,000, 622 branches, and a staff of ... ... had gained a place in the list of the great banks of ...

T. C. Kinnear
President 1869-1870

Thos. Ritchie
Vice-President 1890-1907

Hon. J. Northup
Vice-President 1872-1879

Michael Dwyer
Vice-President 1880-1884

CHRONOLOGY OF
THE ROYAL BANK OF CANADA

1869 Charter of incorporation obtained in the name of the "Merchants Bank of Halifax."
Bank open for business in Halifax, N.S. T. C. Kinnear, first President. George Maclean, Cashier.

1870 Thomas E. Kenny elected President on retirement of T. C. Kinnear.

1882 D. H. Duncan appointed Cashier.

1887 Branch opened in Montreal, Que.

1895 Branch opened in St. John's, Newfoundland.

1897 Branch opened in Vancouver, B.C.

1898 Further branch extension in British Columbia.

1899 E. L. Pease appointed Joint General Manager.
Branch opened in Havana, Cuba.
Agency opened in New York City.

1900 E. L. Pease appointed General Manager, vice D. H. Duncan, retired.

1901 Name of bank changed from the "Merchants Bank of Halifax" to "The Royal Bank of Canada."

1902 Purchase by American capitalists of 5000 shares of stock.

1903 Branch opened in Toronto, Ont.
Purchase of assets of Banco de Oriente, Santiago de Cuba.

1904 Purchase of assets of Banco del Comercio, Havana.
Appointment by Government of Cuba as agent for the distribution of $31,000,000 awarded to the Army of Liberation.

1905 Commission from the Cuban Government to distribute a further sum of $30,000,000, remainder of Army Award.
Dividends made payable quarterly.
Herbert S. Holt (now Sir Herbert Holt and President of the Bank) joined the Board of Directors.

1906 Branch opened in Winnipeg, Man.

1907 Head Office removed from Halifax to Montreal.
H. S. Holt elected Vice-President.
Branch opened at San Juan, Porto Rico.

1908 Thomas E. Kenny, President since 1870, died.
Herbert S. Holt elected President; Edson L. Pease Vice-President.
New Head Office building in Montreal occupied.
Branch opened at Nassau, Bahamas.

1909 Branch opened at Quebec.

1910 Purchase of Union Bank of Halifax.
Branches opened in London, England, and Port of Spain, Trinidad.

1911 Branches established at Kingston, Jamaica, and Bridgetown, Barbados.

1912 Purchase of the Traders Bank of Canada.
Purchase of assets of the Bank of British Honduras.
Business year changed to end November 30, instead of December 31, as formerly.

1914 Purchase of the Bank of British Guiana.

1915 Honor of Knighthood conferred upon the President, Herbert S. Holt.
Branch opened at San José, Costa Rica.

1916 Appointment of Edson L. Pease as Managing-Director and of C. E. Neill as General Manager.
Branch established in Caracas, Venezuela.

1917 Purchase of the Quebec Bank.
Retirement of W. B. Torrance, Superintendent of Branches and Chief Inspector, after thirty years of service.

1918 Purchase of the Northern Crown Bank.
Branch opened in Barcelona, Spain.

1919 The Royal Bank of Canada (France) organized and a branch opened in Paris.
Reciprocal working arrangement entered into with the London County Westminster & Parr's Bank, Ltd., of London, Eng.
Branches opened at Rio de Janeiro, Brazil, Buenos Aires, Argentine, and Montevideo, Uruguay.

ORIGINAL SHAREHOLDERS

OF THE

MERCHANTS BANK OF HALIFAX

OCTOBER, 1869

Acadia Fire Insurance Co.	George Esson	Susan M. Coll
Alexander Anderson	Wm. Esson	Alexander McLeod
Edward Albro & Co.	James Farquhar	Antoinette Nordbeck
J. F. Avery, M.D.	Alexander Forrest	Joseph J. Northup
Rev. Edward Ansell	Charles Fletcher	P. & J. O'Mullin
W. J. Almon, M.D.	G. J. Fluck	Edward O'Brien
Thomas Abbott	Anna B. Fairbanks	Olivia Primrose
John Brookfield	David Frieze	F. G. Parker
Wm. H. Bauld	James F. Forbes	T. R. Patillo
Robt. Boak, Jr.	Alpin Grant	P. Power
Samuel M. Brookfield	John Gibson	James Reeves
James Butler	Wm. Gordon	George Romans
W. L. Black	Peter Grant	D. W. Ross
M. P. Black	John Hopkins	David Stirling
E. K. Brown	Hannah Hopkins	Sircum & Marshall
Thomas Bayne	David Hunter	Wm. J. Stairs
Wm. Boak	James Hunter	Catherine M. Stairs
S. G. Black	Edward Jost	John F. Stairs
Robert Bushell	Alfred G. Jones	Edward Smith
Basil Bell	J. R. Jennett	Edward Smith, Trustee
Stanly Boyd	Edward J. Kenny	Bennett Smith
John Crerar	W. H. Keating	John E. Shatford
W. J. Coleman	E. J. Longard	John A. Sinclair
Miss Jane Cochran	Edward LeGuire	John Starr & G. A. S.
John Costley	W. J. Lewis	Crichton
Frederick Curry	Thos. E. Murphy	John H. Symons
Colin Campbell, Jr.	William MacKay	Rev. J. S. Smith
F. W. Collins	J. K. Munnis	James Scott
Wm. Campbell	John P. Mott	C. E. D. Snow
McB. Campbell	Muir & Blackadar	A. & W. Smith
John Duffus	G. A. McKenzie	Jabeth Snow
R. B. Dickey	Charles H. McKenzie	Lewis A. Sponagle
Wm. Duffus	Roderick McKenzie	James A. Shaw
Rev. H. D. DeBlois	John S. Maclean	James Tupper
Louisa DeGruchy	Rev. P. G. McGregor	Freeman Tupper

James Butler
Vice-President 1885-1890

William Cunard
Director 1860-1871

J. B. Duffus
Director 1869-1870

John Taylor
Director 1860-1876

ORIGINAL SHAREHOLDERS
OF THE
MERCHANTS BANK OF HALIFAX
OCTOBER, 1869

Acadia Fire Insurance Co.
Alexander Anderson
Edward Albro & Co.
J. F. Avery, M.D.
Rev. Edward Ansell
W. J. Almon, M.D.
Thomas Abbott
John Brookfield
Wm. H. Baudd
Robt. Boak, Jr.
Samuel M. Brookfield
James Butler
W. L. Black
M. P. Black
E. K. Brown
Thomas Bayne
Wm. Boak
S. G. Black
Robert Bushell
Basil Bell
Stanly Boyd
John Crerar
W. J. Coleman
Miss Jane Cochran
John Costley
Frederick Curry
Colin Campbell, Jr.
F. W. Collins
Wm. Campbell
McB. Campbell
John Duffus
R. B. Dickey
Wm. Duffus
Rev. H. D. DeBlois
Louisa DeGruchy

George Esson
Wm. Esson
James Farquhar
Alexander Forrest
Charles Fletcher
G. J. Fluck
Anna B. Fairbanks
David Frieze
James F. Forbes
Alpin Grant
John Gibson
Wm. Gordon
Peter Grant
John Hopkins
Hannah Hopkins
David Hunter
James Hunter
Edward Jost
Alfred G. Jones
J. R. Jennett
Edward J. Kenny
W. H. Keating
E. J. Longard
Edward LeGuire
W. J. Lewis
Thos. E. Murphy
William MacKay
J. K. Munnis
John P. Mott
Muir & Blackadar
G. A. McKenzie
Charles H. McKenzie
Roderick McKenzie
John S. Maclean
Rev. P. G. McGregor

Susan M. Coll
Alexander McLeod
Antoinette Nordbeck
Joseph J. Northup
P. & J. O'Mullin
Edward O'Brien
Olivia Primrose
F. G. Parker
T. R. Patillo
P. Power
James Reeves
George Romans
D. W. Ross
David Stirling
Sircum & Marshall
Wm. J. Stairs ·
Catherine M. Stairs
John F. Stairs
Edward Smith
Edward Smith, Trustee
Bennett Smith
John E. Shatford
John A. Sinclair
John Starr & G. A. S.
  Crichton
John H. Symons
Rev. J. S. Smith
James Scott
C. E. D. Snow
A. & W. Smith
Jabeth Snow
Lewis A. Sponagle
James A. Shaw
James Tupper
Freeman Tupper

[36]

James Butler
Vice-President 1885-1890

William Cunard
Director 1869-1871

J. B. Duffus
Director 1869-1870

John Taylor
Director 1869-1878

James Thomson	Cathcart Thomson	Jas. T. West
Wm. Taylor	Joseph Wier	Augustus W. West
Experience Tupper	W. E. Wier	Wm. Cunard
John Thomson	S. A. White	Jas. B. Duffus
Robert Taylor	Mary E. Wilson	Michael Dwyer
James W. Turner	John Watt	Edward Kenny
S. C. Tupper	J. Taylor Wood	Thos. E. Kenny
John Taylor	John L. Whytal	T. C. Kinnear
Harriet A. Taylor	Wm. Whytal & Co.	Jas. W. Merkel
A. D. Thomson	N. L. West	Jeremiah Northup

OFFICERS, 1869-1919

PRESIDENTS

T. C. KINNEAR 1869-1870
T. E. KENNY 1870-1908

H. S. HOLT (Sir Herbert S.
Holt, K.B., 1915) . . 1908

VICE-PRESIDENTS

HON. J. NORTHUP . . . 1872-1879
M. DWYER 1880-1884
JAMES BUTLER. 1885-1890
THOMAS RITCHIE. . . . 1890-1907

H. S. HOLT 1907-1908
E. L. PEASE. 1908
E. F. B. JOHNSTON, K.C.
(2nd Vice-President) 1912-1919

DIRECTORS

T. C. KINNEAR 1869-1870
T. E. KENNY 1869-1908
WILLIAM CUNARD . . . 1869-1871
J. B. DUFFUS 1869-1870
JOHN TAYLOR 1869-1878
M. DWYER 1869-1900
EDWARD SMITH 1869-1870
HON. J. NORTHUP . . . 1870-1879
JOSEPH WIER 1870-1875
J. B. CAMPBELL 1870
T. ABBOTT 1871-1876
JAMES BUTLER. 1871-1890
T. A. RITCHIE 1876-1890
A. BURNS 1876
ALLISON SMITH 1876-1889
J. NORMAN RITCHIE . . 1880-1886
E. J. DAVYS. 1884-1888
THOMAS RITCHIE . . . 1886-1909
WILEY SMITH 1889-1916
H. G. BAULD 1890-1909
H. H. FULLER. 1890-1900
HON. D. MACKEEN . . 1896-1916
H. S. HOLT (Sir Herbert S.
  Holt, K.B., 1915) . . 1905
JAS. REDMOND 1905
F. W. THOMPSON. . . . 1906-1912

E. L. PEASE. 1907
G. R. CROWE 1907
D. K. ELLIOTT. 1907
HON. W. H. THORNE . . 1907
HUGH PATON 1908
T. J. DRUMMOND. . . . 1909-1916
W. B. TORRANCE. . . . 1910
WILLIAM ROBERTSON . . 1910-1919
A. J. BROWN, K.C. . . 1912
E. F. B. JOHNSTON, K.C. 1912-1919
W. J. SHEPPARD 1912
C. S. WILCOX 1912
A. E. DYMENT 1912
C. E. NEILL 1914
MORTIMER B. DAVIS
  (Sir Mortimer B. Davis,
  K.B., 1917) 1916
G. H. DUGGAN 1916
C. C. BLACKADAR . . . 1917
JOHN T. ROSS 1917
R. MACD. PATERSON . . 1917
G. G. STUART, K.C. . . 1917-1918
W. H. MCWILLIAMS . . 1918
CAPT. WM. ROBINSON . 1919
A. MCTAVISH CAMPBELL 1919
ROBERT ADAIR. 1919

CASHIERS

GEORGE MACLEAN . . . 1869-1882

D. H. DUNCAN 1882-1899

GENERAL MANAGERS

E. L. PEASE (MANAGING DIRECTOR, 1916) . . . 1899-1916
C. E. NEILL 1916-

[40]

Edward Smith
Director 1869-1870

Joseph Wier
Director 1870-1875

T.A.Ritchie
Director 1876-1890

OFFICERS, 1869-1919

[40]

Edward Smith
Director 1869-1870

Joseph Wier
Director 1870-1875

T.A.Ritchie
Director 1876-1890

PRESENT OFFICERS OF
THE ROYAL BANK OF CANADA

INCORPORATED 1869   HEAD OFFICE, MONTREAL

Capital Authorized	$25,000,000	Reserve Funds	$ 18,000,000
Capital Paid-up	17,000,000	Total Assets	533,000,000

BOARD OF DIRECTORS

SIR HERBERT S. HOLT, President

E. L. PEASE, Vice-President and Managing Director

JAS. REDMOND, Montreal, Que.

C. E. NEILL, Montreal, Que.

G. R. CROWE, Winnipeg, Man.

SIR MORTIMER B. DAVIS, Montreal, Que.

D. K. ELLIOTT, Winnipeg, Man.

G. H. DUGGAN, Montreal, Que.

HON. W. H. THORNE, St. John, N.B

C. C. BLACKADAR, Halifax, N.S.

HUGH PATON, Montreal, Que.

JOHN T. ROSS, Quebec, Que.

A. J. BROWN, K.C., Montreal, Que.

R. MACD. PATERSON, Montreal, Que.

W. J. SHEPPARD, Waubaushene, Ont.

W. H. McWILLIAMS, Winnipeg, Man.

C. S. WILCOX, Hamilton, Ont.

CAPT. WM. ROBINSON, Winnipeg, Man.

A. E. DYMENT, Toronto, Ont.

A. McTAVISH CAMPBELL, Winnipeg, Man.

ROBERT ADAIR, Montreal, Que.

OFFICERS: HEAD OFFICE

E. L. PEASE, Managing Director

C. E. NEILL, General Manager

F. J. SHERMAN,
    Assistant General Manager

M. W. WILSON,
    Superintendent of Branches

G. W. MACKIMMIE, General Inspector

S. R. NOBLE, General Inspector

S. G. DOBSON, General Inspector

S. D. BOAK, Secretary

L. P. SNYDER, Supervisor of Bank Premises

SUPERVISORS

STUART STRATHY, Supervisor of Ontario Branches

B. B. STEVENSON, Supervisor of Quebec Branches

A. D. McRAE, Supervisor of Maritime Province Branches

R. CAMPBELL, Supervisor of Central Western Branches

C. W. FRAZEE, Supervisor of British Columbia Branches

J. R. BRUCE, Supervisor of General Southern Business

F. J. BEATTY, Supervisor of Cuban Branches

W. A. McKINLAY, Supervisor of Branches in Porto Rico and Venezuela

C. C. PINEO, Supervisor of South American Branches

THE ROYAL BANK OF CANADA

GENERAL STATEMENT

LIABILITIES, NOVEMBER 29, 1919

To the Public: —

Deposits not bearing interest $159,656,229.68
Deposits bearing interest, including interest accrued to date of
 Statement 259,465,169.69

 Total Deposits $419,121,399.37

Notes of the Bank in Circulation 39,837,265.74
Balance due to Dominion Government 14,000,000.00
Balances due to other Banks in Canada 13,970.88
Balances due to Banks and Banking Correspondents in the United
 Kingdom and foreign countries 7,449,852.42
Bills payable 806,776.89
Acceptances under Letters of Credit 16,467,978.69

 $497,697,243.99

To the Shareholders: —

Capital Stock Paid-up $17,000,000.00
Reserve Fund 17,000,000.00
Balance of Profits carried forward 1,096,418.74
Dividends Unclaimed 8,203.08
Dividend No. 129 (at 12% per annum), payable Dec. 1st, 1919 . 505,219.12
Fiftieth Anniversary Bonus of 2%, payable Dec. 20th, 1919 . . 340,000.00

 $533,647,084.93

[44]

THE ROYAL BANK OF CANADA

GENERAL STATEMENT

ASSETS, NOVEMBER 29, 1919

Current Coin	$17,653,879.92
Dominion Notes	26,735,724.00
United States Currency	8,746,805.00
Other Foreign Money	2,545,138.41
Deposit in the Central Gold Reserves	24,500,000.00
Notes of other Banks	3,464,200.00
Cheques on other Banks	23,757,240.33
Balances due by other Banks in Canada	17,103.80
Balances due by Banks and Banking Correspondents elsewhere than in Canada	18,101,373.08
Dominion and Provincial Government Securities, not exceeding market value	45,323,598.66
Canadian Municipal Securities and British, Foreign and Colonial Public Securities other than Canadian, not exceeding market value	33,400,542.77
Railway and other Bonds, Debentures and Stocks, not exceeding market value	19,414,891.06
Call Loans in Canada, on Bonds, Debentures and Stocks	16,435,614.30
Call and Short (not exceeding thirty days) Loans elsewhere than in Canada	33,812,751.53
	$273,908,862.86
Other Current Loans and Discounts in Canada (less rebate of interest)	143,259,518.47
Other Current Loans and Discounts elsewhere than in Canada (less rebate of interest)	90,210,271.33
Overdue Debts (estimated loss provided for)	365,089.66
Real Estate other than Bank Premises	1,495,271.00
Bank Premises, at not more than cost, less amounts written off	7,016,444.12
Liabilities of Customers under Letters of Credit, as per contra	16,467,978.69
Deposit with the Minister for the purposes of the Circulation Fund	750,000.00
Other Assets not included in the foregoing	173,648.80
	$533,647,084.93

H. S. HOLT, *President*   E. L. PEASE, *Managing Director*   C. E. NEILL, *General Manager*

[45]

COMPARATIVE STATEMENT

SHOWING THE PROGRESS OF THE BANK SINCE
INCORPORATION IN 1869

	Capital Paid Up	Reserve Fund	Deposits	Total Loans including Call Loans	Total Assets	Dividends
1869	$ 300,000	$ 20,000	$ 284,656	$ 266,970	$ 729,163	–
1870	400,000	20,000	288,251	791,645	954,160	7½%
1871	400,000	20,000	424,343	1,102,032	1,336,393	7
1872	600,000	60,000	485,732	1,278,850	1,792,386	8
1873	797,920	100,000	779,201	1,870,493	2,391,716	8
1874	800,000	150,000	1,022,024	2,384,148	2,911,839	8
1875	900,000	180,000	869,312	2,201,531	2,594,917	8
1876	900,000	180,000	913,377	2,165,140	2,599,298	8
1877	900,000	180,000	1,290,929	2,382,848	2,963,208	7
1878	900,000	180,000	1,203,373	2,241,354	2,826,423	8
1879	900,000	180,000	1,097,025	2,092,729	2,667,793	7
1880	900,000	180,000	1,232,362	2,086,655	2,874,805	7
1881	900,000	180,000	1,616,090	2,745,156	3,394,669	7
1882	900,000	180,000	1,777,439	3,219,179	3,728,899	7
1883	1,000,000	200,000	1,927,674	3,098,390	4,162,384	7
1884	1,000,000	200,000	2,257,701	3,226,053	4,355,549	7
1885	1,000,000	120,000	1,742,835	2,853,559	3,761,078	6
1886	1,000,000	120,000	1,741,259	2,557,796	3,848,323	6
1887	1,000,000	160,000	2,294,334	3,250,580	4,558,742	6
1888	1,000,000	200,000	2,901,122	3,845,124	5,286,184	6
1889	1,100,000	275,000	2,971,718	4,184,972	5,569,152	6
1890	1,100,000	375,000	3,277,606	4,434,701	5,849,017	6
1891	1,100,000	450,000	3,484,872	4,798,945	6,264,107	6
1892	1,100,000	510,000	4,251,908	5,664,891	7,601,674	6
1893	1,100,000	600,000	4,272,931	5,732,426	7,641,360	6½
1894	1,100,000	680,000	4,966,316	6,327,816	8,538,620	7
1895	1,500,000	975,000	6,199,207	7,135,180	9,811,625	7
1896	1,500,000	1,075,000	6,327,768	7,873,493	10,758,753	7
1897	1,500,000	1,175,000	6,926,816	7,498,109	10,967,413	7
1898	1,500,000	1,250,000	8,275,407	8,498,831	12,681,664	7
1899	1,985,000	1,700,000	11,323,599	11,813,487	17,101,513	7
1900	2,000,000	1,700,000	12,015,710	12,282,096	17,844,038	7
1901	2,000,000	1,700,000	13,363,124	13,260,562	19,376,717	7
1902	2,481,000	2,500,000	13,929,120	14,132,124	21,869,968	7½
1903	3,000,000	3,000,000	16,087,446	16,341,857	25,106,736	8

[46]

Allison Smith
Director 1876 - 1889

J. Norman Ritchie
Director 1880 - 1886

E. J. Davys
Director 1884 - 1888

H. H. Fuller
Director 1889 - 1900

COMPARATIVE STATEMENT

	Capital Paid Up	Reserve Fund	Deposits	Total Loans including Call Loans	Total Assets	Dividends
1869	$ 300,000	$ 20,000	$ 284,656	$ 266,970	$ 729,163	–
1870	400,000	20,000	288,251	791,645	954,160	7½%
1871	400,000	20,000	424,343	1,102,032	1,336,393	7
1872	600,000	60,000	485,732	1,278,850	1,792,386	8
1873	797,920	100,000	779,201	1,870,493	2,391,716	8
1874	800,000	150,000	1,022,024	2,384,148	2,911,839	8
1875	900,000	180,000	869,312	2,201,531	2,594,917	8
1876	900,000	180,000	913,377	2,165,140	2,599,298	8
1877	900,000	180,000	1,290,929	2,382,848	2,963,208	7
1878	900,000	180,000	1,203,373	2,241,354	2,826,423	8
1879	900,000	180,000	1,097,025	2,092,729	2,667,793	7
1880	900,000	180,000	1,232,362	2,086,655	2,874,805	7
1881	900,000	180,000	1,616,090	2,745,156	3,394,669	7
1882	900,000	180,000	1,777,439	3,219,179	3,728,899	7
1883	1,000,000	200,000	1,927,674	3,098,390	4,162,384	7
1884	1,000,000	200,000	2,257,701	3,226,053	4,355,549	7
1885	1,000,000	120,000	1,742,835	2,853,559	3,761,078	6
1886	1,000,000	120,000	1,741,259	2,557,796	3,848,323	6
1887	1,000,000	160,000	2,294,334	3,250,580	4,558,742	6
1888	1,000,000	200,000	2,901,122	3,845,124	5,286,184	6
1889	1,100,000	275,000	2,971,718	4,184,972	5,569,152	6
1890	1,100,000	375,000	3,277,606	4,434,701	5,849,017	6
1891	1,100,000	450,000	3,484,872	4,798,945	6,264,107	6
1892	1,100,000	510,000	4,251,908	5,664,891	7,601,674	6
1893	1,100,000	600,000	4,272,931	5,732,426	7,641,360	6½
1894	1,100,000	680,000	4,966,316	6,327,816	8,538,620	7
1895	1,500,000	975,000	6,199,207	7,135,180	9,811,625	7
1896	1,500,000	1,075,000	6,327,768	7,873,493	10,758,753	7
1897	1,500,000	1,175,000	6,926,816	7,498,109	10,967,413	7
1898	1,500,000	1,250,000	8,275,407	8,498,831	12,681,664	7
1899	1,935,000	1,700,000	11,323,599	11,813,487	17,101,513	7
1900	2,000,000	1,700,000	12,015,710	12,282,096	17,844,038	7
1901	2,000,000	1,700,000	13,363,124	13,260,562	19,376,717	7
1902	2,481,000	2,500,000	13,929,120	14,132,124	21,869,968	7½
1903	3,000,000	3,000,000	16,087,446	16,341,857	25,106,736	8

Allison Smith
Director 1876-1889

J. Norman Ritchie
Director 1880-1886

E. J. Davys
Director 1884-1888

H. H. Fuller
Director 1890-1900

	Capital Paid Up	Reserve Fund	Deposits	Total Loans including Call Loans	Total Assets	Dividends
1904	$3,000,000	$3,000,000	$21,945,144	$18,198,282	$31,183,652	8%
1905	3,000,000	3,400,000	26,435,658	22,497,367	36,373,576	8
1906	3,900,000	4,390,000	32,464,685	28,668,920	45,437,516	9
1907	3,900,000	4,390,000	33,265,498	29,815,562	46,351,498	10
1908	3,900,000	4,600,000	37,443,441	30,660,987	50,470,210	10
1909	5,000,000	5,700,000	50,822,129	43,838,544	67,051,102	10
1910	6,200,000	7,000,000	72,079,607	60,586,264	92,510,346	11
1911	6,251,080	7,056,188	88,294,808	73,630,725	110,528,512	12
1912	11,560,000	12,560,000	137,891,667	124,239,826	179,210,758	12
1913	11,560,000	12,560,000	138,177,662	122,536,348	180,246,785	12
1914	11,560,000	12,560,000	136,051,208	114,811,565	179,404,054	12
1915	11,560,000	12,560,000	154,976,327	126,022,959	198,299,123	12
1916	12,000,000	12,560,000	200,227,595	157,779,331	253,261,427	12
1917	12,911,700	14,000,000	252,987,382	183,226,953	335,574,186	12
1918	14,000,000	15,000,000	332,591,717	218,190,065	427,512,982	12
1919	17,000,000	17,000,000	419,121,399	284,083,245	533,647,084	12*

* And 2% bonus.

BRANCHES OF
THE ROYAL BANK OF CANADA

1869— 1	1882—22	1895—26	1908—107
1870— 2	1883—21	1896—27	1909—124
1871— 7	1884—21	1897—30	1910—174
1872— 8	1885—22	1898—36	1911—202
1873—10 .	1886—23	1899—42	1912—326
1874—11	1887—25	1900—40	
1875—11	1888—25	1901—41	1913—363
1876—11	1889—24	1902—42	1914—379
1877—12	1890—24	1903—46	1915—368
1878—12	1891—24	1904—52	1916—369
1879—12	1892—25	1905—59	1917—422
1880—12	1893—25·	1906—78	1918—524
1881—13	1894—25	1907—94	1919—622

II—BRANCHES AS ON NOVEMBER 30, 1919

IN CANADA AND NEWFOUNDLAND

Ontario	160
Quebec	52
New Brunswick	25
Nova Scotia	65
Prince Edward Island	10
Alberta	41
Manitoba	35
Saskatchewan	104
British Columbia	48
Newfoundland	9
Total Canada and Nfld.	549

FOREIGN

WEST INDIES

Cuba	32
Porto Rico, Dom. Republic and Haiti	9
British West Indies	13
French West Indies	3

CENTRAL & SOUTH AMERICA

Argentine, Brazil, Uruguay	3
Venezuela and British Guiana	7
British Honduras and Costa Rica	2

EUROPE

London, Paris and Barcelona	3

UNITED STATES

New York	1
Total Foreign	73
Total in Canada and Newfoundland	549
GRAND TOTAL	622

BRANCHES OF
THE ROYAL BANK OF CANADA

ONTARIO

APPIN	C.V. McGillivray, Act'g
ARTHUR	W. Pinder
AYLMER	H. E. Armstrong
AYTON	C. S. Campbell
BATH	G. W. Cuppage
BEETON	R. A. O. Hobbes
BELLEVILLE	W. A. Parker
BLIND RIVER	W. L. Simpson
BOWMANVILLE	F. J. Mitchell
BRACEBRIDGE	C. S. Hare
BRANTFORD	P. D. Knowles
BRIDGEBURG	J. R. Steele
BROCKVILLE	I. C. McClean
BROWNSVILLE	V. P. Heppler
BRUCE MINES	W. F. Clark
BURFORD	C. W. Goodman
BURK'S FALLS	A. J. Linton
BURLINGTON	L. H. Hillary
CARGILL	C. R. Davis
CHAPLEAU	H. B. Pelton
CHATHAM	B. M. Green
CHATSWORTH	A. A. Hutchison
CHIPPAWA	L. E. Torey
CLIFFORD	A. S. Winlow
CLINTON	R. E. Manning
COLLINGWOOD	A. Welch
COMBER	C. F. Kennedy
CORNWALL	F. B. Brownridge
DRAYTON	J. J. Davis
DRYDEN	M. D. Hambly
DUNDAS	S. Hughes
DURHAM	J. A. Rowland
DUTTON	G. N. Giddy
ELMIRA	A. E. Herman
ELMWOOD	C. W. Zilliax, Acting
ELORA	N. D. Hall
EMBRO	W. J. Hetherington
EMBRUN	J. A. Lacombe
ENTERPRISE	F. J. Hunter
FERGUS	R. F. Aitchison
FLORENCE	C. N. Sarney
FORT WILLIAM	H. B. Wilson
GALT	Wm. Philip
GLENCOE	G. Dickson
GRAND VALLEY	W. O'C. Ahern
GUELPH	R. L. Torrance
HAILEYBURY	A. G. Kirkpatrick
HAMILTON	R. H. Harvey
	C. A. R. Warren, Asst.
EAST END	J. A. Laird
JOHN STREET	C. I. Lancefield
MARKET BRANCH	A. R. Lancefield
HANOVER	M. J. Muter
HARRISTON	Geo. Murison
HUNTSVILLE	R. F. Grant
INGERSOLL	R. W. Green
INGLEWOOD	A. V. Kellum
INWOOD	M. S. Crawforth
IROQUOIS FALLS	A. J. Kelly
KEEWATIN	F. Bruce
KENORA	J. H. Fraser
KINCARDINE	D. H. Morison
KINGSTON	E. E. Newman
MARKET BRANCH	D. Murray
KITCHENER	F. H. Boehmer
LAKEFIELD	J. B. Jarrell
LAMBETH	G. H. Hardy, Acting
LEAMINGTON	E. M. Sharpe
LINDSAY	H. C. Sootheran
LION'S HEAD	E. Paterson
LONDON	V. F. Cronyn
RICHMOND AND PICCADILLY	R. H. Gale
LONDON EAST	W. D. Beamer
LYNDEN	R. H. Balfour
MALLORYTOWN	W. S. McCauley
MASSEY	W. E. Soule
MERRICKVILLE	F. C. Lorway
MIDLAND	L. T. Brandon
MOREWOOD	J. White
MOUNT FOREST	R. A. Fowlie
MOUNT HAMILTON	R. A. Wallace
NAPANEE	R. G. H. Travers
NIAGARA FALLS	C. E. Brien
NIAGARA FALLS CENTRE	R. M. Wilson
NORTH BAY	J. H. Cummings
NORWICH	R. F. Montgomery
ODESSA	H. Ryckman
ORILLIA	Geo. Rapley

ONTARIO *(Continued)*

OSHAWA	H. C. Lander	THOROLD	Geo. H. Shaw
OTTAWA	C. A. Gray	TILLSONBURG	C. E. Parlow
BANK ST.	Geo. Brownlee	TORONTO	D. C. Rea / A. T. Lowe, Asst.
HINTONBURGH	W. S. Holmes		
MARKET BRANCH	J. P. Prendergast	AVENUE Road	V. U. Heming
RIDEAU ST.	P. B. Taylor	BLOOR AND	
OTTERVILLE	A. M. Bryson	DOVERCOURT	E. S. Crocker
OWEN SOUND	E. A. Batcheller	CEDARVALE	B. C. Stone
PAISLEY	T. R. McLennan	CHURCH ST.	W. F. Brock
PEMBROKE	R. L. McCormick	COLLEGE AND	
PERTH	E. M. Doull	BATHURST	G. W. Roberts
PETERBOROUGH	V. Eastwood	DANFORTH AVE.	R. O. Darling
PORT ARTHUR	J. A. Macarthur	DUNDAS AND	
PORT DOVER	C. P. Freeman	CHESTNUT	D. I. Asling
PORT HOPE	W. H. Roper	GERRARD AND JONES	T. G. Haslam
PORT McNICOLL	Lloyd Porter, Acting	GERRARD AND	
PRESCOTT	T. H. Pringle	LOGAN	F. E. London
RIDGETOWN	A. Pow	KEELE AND	
RIPLEY	W. O. Jackson	ST. CLAIR	J. P. Denneny
ROCKWOOD	G. R. Martin	KING AND SPADINA	K. D. Simpson
RODNEY	W. E. Hanley	QUEEN AND	
ST. CATHARINES	D. Muir	BROADVIEW	G. M. Baines
ST. MARY'S	J. Pool	RUNNYMEDE AND	
ST. THOMAS	J. A. Elliott	BLOOR	B. N. Britton
SARNIA	W. G. Turnbull	SPADINA AND	
SAULT STE. MARIE	A. G. Knowles	COLLEGE	H. V. Maynard
QUEEN AND BRUCE		YONGE AND BLOOR	R. P. Sherris
STREETS	J. D. Tipton	YONGE AND COLLEGE	R. B. Caldwell
STEELTON BRANCH	R. E. Culbert	YONGE AND	
SCHOMBERG	H. C. Bowerman	RICHMOND	P. A. Vale
SCOTLAND	H. B. Sutherland	TOTTENHAM	I. N. Tompkins
SEELEY'S BAY	A. H. Votier	TWEED	M. E. McKenzie
SIMCOE	T. Muir	VARS	E. G. Bethel
SOUTH RIVER	W. P. Spero	WARDSVILLE	G. A. Love
SPENCERVILLE	W. J. Nicholson	WATERDOWN	W. J. Wiggins
SPRINGFIELD	Geo. Stewart	WATERLOO	H. G. Mistele
STONEY CREEK	C. D. Wells	WEBBWOOD	J. E. Neill
STRATFORD	S. B. Martin	WELLAND	H. B. H. Macgowan
STRATHROY	F. P. Hughes	WEST FORT WILLIAM	H. E. Girvan
STURGEON FALLS	L. J. Gilleland	WINDSOR	Geo. Mair
SUDBURY	C. W. Morris	WINONA	C. D. Wells
THAMESFORD	J. O. Otterbein	WOODBRIDGE	J. G. Hallett
		WOODSTOCK	C. H. McDunnough

Wiley Smith
Director 1889-1916

Hon. D. Mac Keen
Director 1896-1916

D. H. Duncan
Cashier 1882-1899

K. G. Bauld
Director 1890-1909

ONTARIO (Continued)

OSHAWA	H. C. Lander
OTTAWA	C. A. Gray
BANK ST	Geo. Brownlee
HINTONBURGH	W. S. Holmes
MARKET BRANCH	J. P. Prendergast
RIDEAU ST	P. B. Taylor
OTTERVILLE	A. M. Bryson
OWEN SOUND	E. A. Batcheller
PAISLEY	T. R. McLennan
PEMBROKE	R. L. McCormick
PERTH	E. M. Doull
PETERBOROUGH	V. Eastwood
PORT ARTHUR	J. A. Macarthur
PORT DOVER	C. P. Freeman
PORT HOPE	W. H. Roper
PORT McNICOLL	Lloyd Porter, Acting
PRESCOTT	T. H. Pringle
RIDGETOWN	A. Pow
RIPLEY	W. O. Jackson
ROCKWOOD	G. R. Martin
RODNEY	W. E. Hanley
ST. CATHARINES	D. Muir
ST. MARY'S	J. Pool
ST. THOMAS	J. A. Elliott
SARNIA	W. G. Turnbull
SAULT STE. MARIE	A. G. Knowles
QUEEN AND BRUCE STREETS	J. D. Tipton
STEELTON BRANCH	R. E. Culbert
SCHOMBERG	H. C. Bowerman
SCOTLAND	H. B. Sutherland
SEELEY'S BAY	A. H. Votier
SIMCOE	T. Muir
SOUTH RIVER	W. P. Spero
SPENCERVILLE	W. J. Nicholson
SPRINGFIELD	Geo. Stewart
STONEY CREEK	C. D. Wells
STRATFORD	S. B. Martin
STRATHROY	F. P. Hughes
STURGEON FALLS	L. J. Gilleland
SUDBURY	C. W. Morris
THAMESFORD	J. O. Otterbein

THOROLD	Geo. H. Shaw
TILLSONBURG	C. E. Parlow
TORONTO	D. C. Rea / A. T. Lowe, Asst.
AVENUE Road	V. U. Heming
BLOOR AND DOVERCOURT	E. S. Crocker
CEDARVALE	B. C. Stone
CHURCH ST	W. F. Brock
COLLEGE AND BATHURST	G. W. Roberts
DANFORTH AVE	R. O. Darling
DUNDAS AND CHESTNUT	D. I. Asling
GERRARD AND JONES	T. G. Haslam
GERRARD AND LOGAN	F. E. London
KEELE AND ST. CLAIR	J. P. Denneny
KING AND SPADINA	K. D. Simpson
QUEEN AND BROADVIEW	G. M. Baines
RUNNYMEDE AND BLOOR	B. N. Britton
SPADINA AND COLLEGE	H. V. Maynard
YONGE AND BLOOR	R. P. Sherris
YONGE AND COLLEGE	R. B. Caldwell
YONGE AND RICHMOND	P. A. Vale
TOTTENHAM	I. N. Tompkins
TWEED	M. E. McKenzie
VARS	E. G. Bethel
WARDSVILLE	G. A. Love
WATERDOWN	W. J. Wiggins
WATERLOO	H. G. Mistele
WEARNWOOD	J. E. Neill
WELLAND	H. B. H. Macgowan
WEST FORT WILLIAM	H. E. Girvan
WINGER	Geo. Mair
WROXA	C. D. Wells
WINDRIDGE	J. G. Hallett
WOODSTOCK	C. H. McDunnough

{ 52 }

Wiley Smith
Director 1889-1916

Hon. D. MacKeen
Director 1896-1916

D. H. Duncan
Cashier 1882-1899

H. G. Bauld
Director 1890-1909

THE ROYAL BANK OF CANADA

SUB-BRANCHES IN ONTARIO

ALDERSHOT
Sub-branch to Hamilton Market. Open Tuesday and Friday

ALMA
Sub-branch to Elora. Open Wednesday and Saturday

AVON
Sub-branch to Springfield. Open Monday, Wednesday and Friday

BURGESSVILLE
Sub-branch to Norwich. Open Tuesday and Friday

BURRITT'S RAPIDS
Sub-branch to Merrickville. Open Daily

CHELTENHAM
Sub-branch to Inglewood. Open Monday

COPETOWN
Sub branch to Lynden. Open Tuesday and Thursday

CORINTH
Sub-branch to Brownsville. Open Monday and Friday

ESPANOLA
Sub-branch to Webbwood. Open Tuesday and Friday

KEARNEY
Sub-branch to Burk's Falls. Open Wednesday

KINTORE
Sub-branch to Thamesford. Open Tuesday and Friday

MOUNT ELGIN
Sub-branch to Ingersoll. Open Daily

NAVAN
Sub-branch to Vars. Open Thursday

PUTNAM
Sub-branch to Ingersoll. Open Wednesday

SUNDRIDGE
Sub-branch to South River. Open Tuesday and Friday

QUEBEC

BLACK LAKE	E. P. Weary
COATICOOK	G. A. Sanford
GRANBY	J. O. Asselin
INVERNESS	W. H. Rothera
JOLIETTE	J. H. Lippé
LA TUQUE	R. Babineau
LENNOXVILLE	R. G. Ward
LONGUEUIL	J. C. Barnes, Acting
MONTMAGNY	L. Tetu
MONTREAL	R. L. Ritchie / J. A. Taylor, Asst.
AMHERST AND ONTARIO	G. LaMothe, Acting
AMHERST AND ST. CATHERINE	J. H. Bender
ATWATER AVE.	J. A. Massicotte
BEAVER HALL	W. H. Stevens
BONAVENTURE	A. T. Tremaine
BONSECOURS MARKET	J. E. Trottier
COTE ST. PAUL	M. Leroux
LAURIER AVE.	H. J. Bulley
PAPINEAU AVE.	W. J. Barry'
PLACE D'ARMES	F. E. Smith
ST. CATHERINE AND BLEURY	A. D. Munro

MONTREAL (*Continued*)	
ST. DENIS AND ST. CATHERINE	A. R. Lafleche
ST. MATTHEW	M. P. Hickson
ST. ZOTIQUE	F. P. Sexton
SEIGNEURS ST.	J. W. Fulton
SHERBROOKE AND BLEURY	R. L. Torrance
SHERBROOKE AND DRAPER	W. T. Turner
STANLEY ST.	J. J. Keyes
VAN HORNE AVE.	A. G. Hooper
MONTREAL WEST	A. W. Allan
PONT ROUGE	D. H. Lamarche
PRINCEVILLE	J. A. Frechette
QUEBEC	A. J. Welch
LIMOILOU	L. J. Robichaud
ST. JOHN ST	A. H. Bisset
ST. ROCH	A. Geo. Russell
ST. SAUVEUR	J. L. Gauthier
UPPER TOWN	C. C. Smith
RAWDON	J. St. Maurice
ROCK ISLAND	A. C. McPhee
ST. GEORGE EAST, BEAUCE	D. A. Bisson

QUEBEC (Continued)

St. Johns............F. Camaraire
St. Lambert.........C. T. Medlar
St. Romuald.........J. A. Lacroix
Shawinigan Falls....O. C. Weary
St. Marc
  (Shawinigan Falls) O. C. Weary

Sherbrooke.........J. M. Phelan
Upper Town.......H. M. Cormier
Thetford Mines.....J. A. McKendy
Three Rivers........G. S. F. Robitaille
Westmount,
  Greene Ave.......Geo. Kydd
  Victoria Ave......C. V. Lindsay

SUB-BRANCHES

Fitch Bay, Sub-branch to Rock Island. Open Thursday

Greenfield Park
Sub-branch to St. Lambert. Open Monday,
Wednesday and Friday

Leeds Village
Sub-branch to Inverness. Open Wednesday
and Saturday

NEW BRUNSWICK

Bathurst............F. H. Eaton
Blackville.........L. G. Fraser
Buctouche.........A. L. Fournier
Campbellton.......J. G. Christie
Canterbury.........H. W. Ferguson, Act'g
Dalhousie..........W. A. R. Cragg
Dorchester........A. V. Smith
Edmundston.........T. J. Scott
Fredericton.........G. A. Taylor
Fredericton
  Junction..........J. C. Cook
Grand Falls.........J. A. McKendy
Harvey Station......W.R.Cruikshank, Act'g

Moncton...........W. C. Hazen
  St. George St......F. C. Dickie
Newcastle.........E. A. McCurdy
Plaster Rock.......H. F. Henderson
Rexton.............R. T. Moseley
Richibucto.........G. O. Long
St. John.............R. E. Smith
  North End.......H. T. Huston
St. Leonards........M. F. White
St. Stephen.........D. C. Davidson
Sackville..........G. H. Mackenzie
Sussex..............W. S. Hay
Woodstock..........C. O. MacDonald

NOVA SCOTIA

Amherst............T. C. Douglas
Annapolis Royal.....H. J. Armstrong
Antigonish.........W. M. Simpson
Arichat............H. A. Tuttle
Baddeck............H. G. Bowes
Barrington Passage..C. J. Durling
Bear River.........W. M. Romans
Berwick.............J. R. Frizzle
Bridgetown........A. F. Little
Bridgewater........H. L. Bentley
Church Point........L. J. Robichaud
Clarke's Harbour...W. G. Keaney
Dartmouth.........J. W. Douglas

Digby ....P. C. R. Harris
Eastern Harbour....A. T. Boudreau, Act'g
Glace Bay..........R. J. M. Cullen
Great Village.......J. L. Snook
Guysboro..........L. H. Potter
Halifax.............B. L. Mitchell, Acting
  Bloomfield........W. D. Melvin
  Buckingham St....R. V. Dimock
  Gottingen St......F. T. Palfrey
  North and Windsor
    Streets.........R. St. C. Hopgood
  Quinpool Road....F. L. Crockett
  Spring Garden
    Road............G. E. Mahon

[56]

F. W. Thompson
Director 1906 - 1912

G. R. Crowe
Director since 1907

D. K. Elliott
Director since 1907

T. J. Drummond
Director 1906 - 1916

Q· ÉBEC (Continued)

St. Johns	F. Camaraire	Sherbrooke	J. M. Phelan
St. Lambert	C. T. Medlar	Upper Town	H. M. Cormier
St. Romuald	J. A. Lacroix	Thetford Mines	J. A. McKendy
Shawinigan Falls	O. C. Weary	Three Rivers	C. S. F. Robitaille
St. Marc		Westmount,	
(Shawinigan Falls)	O. C. Weary	Greene Ave	Geo. Kydd
		Victoria Ave	C. V. Lindsay

SUB-BRANCHES

Fitch Bay, Sub-branch to Rock Island. Open Thursday

GREENFIELD PARK
Sub-branch to St. Lambert. Open Monday, Wednesday and Friday

LEEDS VILLAGE
Sub-branch to Inverness. Open Wednesday and Saturday

NEW BRUNSWICK

Bathurst	F. H. Eaton	Moncton	W. C. Hazen
Blackville	L. G. Fraser	St. George St	F. C. Dickle
Buctouche	A. L. Fournier	Newcastle	E. A. McCurdy
Campbellton	J. G. Christie	Plaster Rock	H. F. Henderson
Canterbury	H. W. Ferguson, Act'g	Rexton	R. T. Moseley
Dalhousie	W. A. R. Cragg	Richibucto	G. O. Long
Dorchester	A. V. Smith	St. John	R. E. Smith
Edmundston	T. J. Scott	North End	H. T. Huston
Fredericton	G. A. Taylor	St. Leonards	M. F. White
Fredericton		St. Stephen	D. C. Davidson
Junction	J. C. Cook	Sackville	G. H. Mackenzie
Grand Falls	J. A. McKendy	Sussex	W. S. Hay
Harvey Station	W.R.Cruikshank, Act'g	Woodstock	C. O. MacDonald

NOVA SCOTIA

Amherst	T. C. Douglas	Digby	P. C. R. Harris
Annapolis Royal	H. J. Armstrong	Eastern Harbour	A. T. Boudreau, Act'g
Antigonish	W. M. Simpson	Glace Bay	R. J. M. Cullen
Arichat	H. A. Tuttle	Great Village	L. L. Soook
Baddeck	H. G. Bowes	Guysboro	L. H. Potter
Barrington Passage	C. J. Durling	Halifax	R. L. Mitchell, Acting
Bear River	W. M. Romans	Blockfield	W. D. Melvin
Berwick	J. R. Frizzle	Buckingham St	R. V. Dimock
Bridgetown	A. F. Little	Gottingen St	P. T. Palfrey
Bridgewater	H. L. Bentley	North and Windsor	
Church Point	L. J. Robichaud	Streets	R. St. C. Hopgood
Clarke's Harbour	W. G. Kenney	Quinpool Road	F. L. Crockett
Dartmouth	J. W. Douglas	Spring Garden	
		Road	G. E. Mahon

F.W. Thompson
Director 1906 - 1912

G. R. Crowe
Director since 1907

D . K. Elliott
Director since 1907

T.J.Drummond
Director 1909 - 1916

NOVA SCOTIA (Continued)

IMPEROYAL..........J. K. McKenzie	NORTH SYDNEY.......H. W. Jubien
INVERNESS..........R. H. Ells	PARRSBORO..........H. E. Mosher
KENTVILLE..........A. A. Thomson	PICTOU..............P. A. Curry
LA HAVE.............A. R. Pringle	PORT HAWKESBURY....J. A. McIsaac
LAWRENCETOWN......F. G. Palfrey	PORT WILLIAMS.......R. S. Hocken
LIVERPOOL..........E. B. McDaniel	ST. PETER'S..........W. L. Wright
LOCKEPORT..........C. K. Hogg	SHERBROOKE........G. L. Capstick
LONDONDERRY.......A. F. Macdonald	SHUBENACADIE.......W. D. Bowers
LOUISBURG..........J. H. Edsall, Acting	SPRINGHILL..........R. W. Wright
LUNENBURG.........R. S. Currie	STEWIACKE..........C. E. Rhind
MABOU..............J. S. Coffey	SYDNEY.............P. G. Hall
MAITLAND..........T. A. Fraser	SYDNEY MINES.......W. D. McMullin
MARBLE MOUNTAIN...A. F. McAlpine	TRURO.............{M. Dickie / L. M. Nicholls, Asst.
METEGHAN RIVER.....W. J. Theriault, Sub.	
MIDDLE	WATERVILLE.........E. G. MacMinn
MUSQUODOBOIT.....R. C. Fraser	WEYMOUTH..........H. M. Doull
MIDDLETON..........J. H. McDaniel	WHITNEY PIER........R. Fash
MULGRAVE..........B. W. Hutchinson	WHYCOCOMAGH......W. P. Robertson
NEW GERMANY.......G. K. Hammett	WINDSOR.............R. C. Wright
NEW GLASGOW.......C. E. McLaggan	WOLFVILLE..........R. Creighton
NEW WATERFORD.....S. A. Morley	YARMOUTH..........F. Shute

PRINCE EDWARD ISLAND

CARDIGAN............M. G. Nickerson	MURRAY RIVER.......L. W. Dickie
CHARLOTTETOWN......A. W. Hyndman	SUMMERSIDE..........R. B. Richardson
ELDON..............F. E. Manson	TIGNISH.............P. Noonan
HUNTER RIVER.......R. H. Pethick	TYNE VALLEY........W. C. Pridham
MOUNT STEWART.....S. M. Daniel	WELLINGTON........J. I. McIntyre, Acting

SUB-BRANCH

RUSTICO, Sub-branch to Hunter River. Open Monday and Thursday

ALBERTA

BEISEKER............A. P. Henry, Acting	CRAIGMYLE..........E. M. Wegren
BIG VALLEY.........A. E. Morrison	DIDSBURY...........J. H. Lowrie
BLUESKY.............F. G. Hamilton	DONNELLY..........P. J. LeMasurier
BRUCE..............J. P. Bush, Sub. Mgr.	EDMONTON........{J. F. McMillan / H. H. Richards, Asst:
CALGARY..........{J. A. Walker / J. G. Nickerson, Asst.	
	SOUTH.............E. G. Sampson
3RD ST. WEST......A. H. Kelly	ERSKINE.............T. W. Boyer
CAMROSE............R. R. Gilbert	GADSBY.............R. W. Stowell
CARDSTON..,.........W. R. Mackay	GLEICHEN...........D. Hutcheson
CASTOR.............R. J. Gregson	HALKIRK............A. J. Cameron, Acting
CLYDE..............F. J. Gant	HIGH RIVER.........M. E. Gray

ALBERTA (*Continued*)

HOLDEN	G. E. McVittie	PEACE RIVER	J. D. Hamilton
KINSELLA	H. J. Nicholson	PICARDVILLE	D. Mackie, Acting
LACOMBE	E. C. Chapman	REDCLIFF	H. W. Harper
LAVOY	A. P. Wilson, Acting	RED DEER	J. M. Campbell
LETHBRIDGE	R. M. Hanson	RED WILLOW	M. H. Gilmour, Sub.
MAGRATH	J. K. Atkinson	ROUND HILL	T. S. Buckham
MEDICINE HAT	R. H. Frazee	RYLEY	D. A. MacNeill, Act'g
MEETING CREEK	D. S. Allan, Acting	STETTLER	W. J. O'Callaghan
MIRROR	F. E. Murray	TABER	J. W. Doran
MORINVILLE	D. A. McMillan	VERMILION	H. R. Calvert
MUNSON	H. W. Hutchings		

SUB-BRANCHES

BUSBY
Sub-branch to Picardville. Open Monday, Wednesday and Friday

HAY LAKES
Sub-branch to Edmonton South. Open Tuesday and Thursday

JARROW
Sub-branch to Kinsella. Open Monday, Wednesday and Friday

RANFURLY
Sub-branch to Lavoy. Open Monday, Wednesday and Friday

SCOLLARD, Sub-branch to Big Valley. Open Wednesday

MANITOBA

ARDEN	C. F. Johnston	STE. ROSE DU LAC	J. Valcourt
BEAUSEJOUR	H. C. Chapin	SHOAL LAKE	A. E. Sharpe
BEULAH	C. Lamb	SOMERSET	W. A. Rowat
BINSCARTH	R. H. Lacey	SPERLING	E. R. Thorburne
BRANDON	W. T. Fyfe	STEINBACH	J. MacPhail
CRANDALL	N. H. Haworth	STONEWALL	H. W. Stephen
ERICKSON	E. M. O'Donnell, Act'g	TILSTON	C. W. Ketcheson, Act'g
GLENBORO	A. C Gibson	WINNIPEG	C. F. Pentland / S. J. Macleod, Asst.
ISABELLA	J. D. Harrower, Act'g		
LANGRUTH	T. D. Holloway	ELMWOOD	R. C. Davison
LA RIVIERE	R. W Behrens	GRAIN EXCHANGE	R. G. Baird
LUNDAR	G Finnbogason, Act'g	MAIN AND LOGAN	M. A. O'Hara
MELITA	C. H. L. Smith	MAIN AND SELKIRK	F. A. Dechman
MINIOTA	H. M. McCallum	PORTAGE AVE	F. W. Doherty
PIERSON	J. A. McIntyre	PORTAGE AND	
PIPESTONE	W. H. Kellum	SHERBROOKE	R. L. Paterson
PLUMAS	A. G. Baxter	SARGENT AVE	F. Thordarson
RATHWELL	G. H. Yule	WILLIAM AND	
ST. BONIFACE	E. S. Phillips	SHERBROOKE	T. E. Thorsteinson

The Royal Bank of Canada

SUB-BRANCHES IN MANITOBA

AMARANTH
Sub-branch to Langruth. Open Wednesday, Thursday and Friday

BALMORAL
Sub-branch to Stonewall. Open Monday, Wednesday and Friday

LAC DU BONNET
Sub-branch to Beausejour. Open Tuesday and Friday

MAGNET
Sub-branch to Ste. Rose du Lac.

MULVIHILL
Sub-branch to Lundar. Open Thursday and Friday

WHITEMOUTH
Sub-branch to Beausejour. Open Wednesday and Saturday

SASKATCHEWAN

ALAMEDA............A. H. Davey	GRAYSON............F.G.Beauchamp,Act'g
ALLAN...............R. W. Hicks	HANLEY..............H. H. Tate
ANEROID.............A. W. Gunn	HARRIS..............A. S. Young
ARDATH..............F. Wood, Acting	HERSCHEL............W. Buck
ATWATER.............D. F. Duke	HOLDFAST............J. M. Bernuy
AYLESBURY...........P. H. Playfair, Acting	IMPERIAL............O. L. Carey
BALCARRES...........E. H. Pringle	INVERMAY............H. S. F. Cunningham
BETHUNE.............R. H. Lockward	KENASTON...........E. Austman
BIGGAR..............L. W. Lyons	KINLEY..............J. A. Wilton
BLADWORTH..........Jas. Gavin	LANCER..............J. E. Tanner
BORDEN..............T.B.Armstrong,Act'g	LANGHAM............J. S. Uren
BROCK...............H. Mackenzie	LAURA...............G. G. Howard
CADILLAC............J. L. McNabb	LEASK...............L. P. Grondines, Act'g
CHAMBERLAIN........H. W. Wilson, Sub.	LEIPZIG..............J. M. Holst
CONQUEST............C.G.M.McBey,Act'g	LIBERTY.............N. V. Coombes
CRAIK...............C. A. Sneath	LINTLAW ............F.C.Kennedy, Acting
CUPAR...............L. C. McKinley	LIPTON..............C. F. Nicholl
DALMENY............J. J. Rempel, Sub.	LLOYDMINSTER.......A. W. Seath
DAVIDSON...........J. H. Hunter	LOCKWOOD...........W. B. Sloan
DELISLE.............Jas. F. McMillan	LUMSDEN............M. M. Barrett
DENZIL..............R. G. Haddow	MACOUN............H. Westergaard
DODSLAND...........I. A. Joudrey	MANOR..............W. H. Bagot
DUBUC...............R. M. Sutherland	MARENGO...........A. J. Trueb
DUNBLANE...........S. A. Maddocks	MARGO..............M. Andrew, Acting
DUNDURN...........H. C. Kent	MARKINCH..........H. Allison
DUVAL..............T. A. Arnott	MARQUIS............N. D. Livingstone
DYSART.............A. McAllan, Acting	MAYMONT...........B. S. Griffin
EARL GREY.........J. O. Spence	MILDEN..............L. A. Carley
ELROSE.............R. S. Macdonald	MOOSE JAW.........F. M. Hughes
FLEMING.............C. H. Wilson	NEVILLE.............H. W. Henderson
FOAM LAKE.........A. Cumming	NOKOMIS............E. C. Wilson
FORGET.............S. Ferguson	NORTH BATTLEFORD...E. Bradish
GLEN EWEN.........V. C. Farrow	PENZANCE...........F. Brown, Acting
GOVAN..............H. H. Ingram	PLATO..............D. Campbell

SASKATCHEWAN *(Continued)*

PONTEIX	T. Adamson	SOVEREIGN	W. J. Laurie
PORTREEVE	G. G. Sinclair	SPY HILL	D. V. Harber
PRELATE	R. Bellinger	STALWART	E. E. Hoare, Acting
PRINCE ALBERT	F. Taylor	STOCKHOLM	N. Calvert
QU'APPELLE	E. F. Dyer	STORNOWAY	D. E. Patterson
QUILL LAKE	O. F. Springer	STORTHOAKS	W. J. Coombes, Act'g
REGINA	W. G. Yule	STRASBOURG	F. L. Screech
NORTH END	H. G. Lyons	SUCCESS	W. L. Barker
ROCKHAVEN	R. Fawcett	SWANSON	H. K. Stopford, Act'g
ROSETOWN	A. C. Thompson	SWIFT CURRENT	E. G. Sampson
RUSH LAKE	F. Kennett	UNITY	C. W. McCallum
SALTCOATS	J. A. Hale	VENN	N. Tamblyn
SASKATOON	F. G. Depew	VISCOUNT	R. C. Forrest
NUTANA	G. R. Chisholm	WALDECK	H. C. Macdonald
SCOTSGUARD	J. J. Black	WEYBURN	F. J. A. Pool
SCOTT	K. V. Bethel	YORKTON	C. H. McIntosh
SEDLEY	A. D. Leslie	YOUNG	James Borrowman
SHEHO	W. M. Gilbert	ZEALANDIA	A. Kennett

SUB-BRANCHES

BIRSAY
Sub-branch to Dunblane. Open Tuesday and Thursday

BRADWELL
Sub-branch to Allan. Open Tuesday and Friday

CLAIR
Sub-branch to Quill Lake. Open Daily

DONAVON
Sub-branch to Delisle. Open Wednesday and Thursday

INSINGER
Sub-branch to Yorkton. Open Monday, Wednesday and Friday

PLUNKETT
Sub-branch to Viscount. Open Tuesday and Thursday

REVENUE
Sub-branch to Scott. Open Friday

SUTHERLAND
Sub-branch to Nutana. Open Tuesday and Friday, also 15th and 16th of Month

WARTIME
Sub-branch to Elrose. Open Tuesday and Friday

ZELMA
Sub-branch to Young. Open Tuesday and Friday

BRITISH COLUMBIA

ABBOTSFORD	N. Hill	KELOWNA	H. F. Rees
ASHCROFT	W. Eadie	LADNER	Jas. Grisdale
BURNS LAKE	M. Henderson, Acting	LADYSMITH	E. J. Johnston
CHILLIWACK	F. B. Lyle	LANGLEY PRAIRIE	H. J. de Canonville, Act'g
COURTENAY	G. F. Marsh	LUMBY	Jas. Baxter
CRANBROOK	F. E. Robertson	MARPOLE	Geo. P. Thorne
CUMBERLAND	F. A. McCarthy	NANAIMO	F. A. Hanna
GRAND FORKS	G. A. Spink	NELSON	A. D. McLeod
KAMLOOPS	G. M. Sinclair	NEW WESTMINSTER	G. H. Stevens

A.J. Brown, K.C.
Director since 1912

Sir Mortimer B. Davis, K.T.
Director since 1916

Hugh Paton
Director since 1908

G.H. Duggan
Director since 1916

SASKATCHEWAN (Continued)

.........T. Adamson	SOVEREIGN............W. J. Laurie
r ....G. G. Sinclair	SPY HILL. ....D. V. Harber
.........R. Bellinger	STALWART............E. E. Hoare, Acting
LRSRT.......F. Taylor	STOCKHOLM...........N. Calvert
F.........E. F. Dyer	STORNOWAY.........D. E. Patterson
.F ....O. F. Springer	STORTHOAKS..........W. J. Coombes, Act'g
.........W. G. Yule	STRASBOURG.........F. L. Screech
END.......H. G. Lyons	SUCCESS............W. L. Barker
EN.........R. Fawcett	SWANSON............H. K. Stopford, Act'g
N. ....A. C. Thompson	SWIFT CURRENT.....E. G. Sampson
KE.......F. Kennett	UNITY...............C. W. McCallum
S. ....J. A. Hale	VENN...............N. Tamblyn
N ....F. G. Depew	VISCOUNT...........R. C. Forrest
.....G. R. Crichton	WALDECK............H. C. Macdonald
KD... .....J. J. Black	WEYBURN...........F. J. A. Pool
.....K. V. Bethel	YORKTON............C. H. McIntosh
.. . A. D. LeCe	YOUNG.......... ...James Borrowman
..... . W. M. Gilbert	ZEALANDIA...........A. Kennett

SUB-BRANCHES

PLUNKETT
ranch to Dunblane. Open Tuesday
Thursday
Sub-branch to Viscount. Open Tuesday
and Thursday

LL
branch to Allan. Open Tuesday and
y
REVENUE
Sub-branch to Scott. Open Friday

branch to Quill Lake. Open Daily
SUTHERLAND
Sub-branch to Nutana. Open Tuesday and
Friday, also 15th and 16th of Month

branch to Delisle. Open Wednesday
Thursday
WARTIME
Sub-branch to Elrose. Open Tuesday and
Friday

branch to Yorkton. Open Monday,
nesday and Friday
ZELMA
Sub-branch to Young. Open Tuesday and
Friday

BRITISH COLUMBIA

SFORD ....N. Hill	KELOWNA,........ ...H. F. Ross,
OFT .. ....W. Eadie	LADNER....... ......Jas. Grisdale
LOU ..... .M. Henderson, Acting	LADYSMITH...........E. J. Johnston
RACE .. ....F B. Lyle	LANGLEY PRAIRIE.....H.J.deCanonville,Act'g
ENAY .... G. F. Marsh	LUMBY...............Jas. Baxter
R N .... .F. E. Robertson	MARPOLE............Geo. P. Thorne
RAND ....F. A. McCarthy	NANAIMO............F. A. Hanna
FORKS.......G. A. Spink	NELSON..,..........A. D. McLeod
PS,.........G. M. Sinclair	NEW WESTMINSTER...G. H. Stevens

A.J. Brown. K.C.
Director since 1912

Sir Mortimer B. Davis. K.B.
Director since 1916

Hugh Paton
Director since 1908

G.H. Duggan
Director since 1916

THE ROYAL BANK OF CANADA

BRITISH COLUMBIA (Continued)

NORTH VANCOUVER....W. Dickinson
PEACHLAND.........M. D. Ross, Acting
PORT ALBERNI.......F. C. Birks
PORT COQUITLAM.....M. S. Kydd
PORT MOODY.........H. Williams
PRINCE GEORGE......W. L. Hornsby
PRINCE RUPERT.......A. W. Cameron
QUESNEL.............D. R. Kelly
ROSSLAND...........E. J. Vanderwater
STEVESTON...........L. Caldecott
TELKWA.............O. H. Wall, Acting
UNION BAY...........M. H. Thomas
VANCOUVER........{Thos. Peacock / R. M. Boyd, Asst.
BRIDGE ST.........C. E. Bourne
CORDOVA ST.......R. Christie

VANCOUVER (Continued)
DAVIE ST..........J. F. M. Pinkham
EAST END.........{S. G. Jardine / H. L. Fraser, Asst.
FAIRVIEW..........H. C. Hopgood
GRANDVIEW........J. W. Logan
HILLCREST.........F. Bosworth
KINGSWAY.........P. A. Anderson, Act'g
KITSILANO.........W. Reid, Acting
MT. PLEASANT.....L. M. Richardson
ROBSON ST........H. C. Seaman
25TH AVE.........P. E. Bradley, Acting
VERNON...........W. A. Butchart
VICTORIA.............A. R. Heiter
DOUGLAS ST.......H. J. Ketchen
FORT ST............W. B. Boucher
VICTORIA WEST.......H. B. Witter

SUB-BRANCH

MILNER, Sub-branch to Langley Prairie. Open Monday, Wednesday and Friday

NEWFOUNDLAND

CAPE BROYLE........P. R. O'Reilly
HARBOR BUFFETT.....P. J. Clarkin
HEARTS CONTENT....P. G. Ledingham, Act'g
MARYSTOWN..........A. White
PLACENTIA..........J. E. Williston

ROSE BLANCHE.......P. Fowler
ST. JOHN'S...........C. E. Jubien
WEST END.........A. Marshall
TRINITY.............S. A. Rafuse

WEST INDIES

CUBA

ANTILLA.............F. J. Tobin
BANES..............C. J. Prangley
BAYAMO............T. Gomar
CAIBARIEN..........S. Echeveste
CAMAGUEY..........A. M. Connolly
AVALLANEDA.......R. D. Socarras
CAMAJUANI..........A. Rangel, Sub.
CARDENAS..........G. Robau
CIEGO DE AVILA......{W. M. Thomson / R. O. Binet, Assistant
CIENFUEGOS.........{A. de Villegas / R. Rangel, Assistant
CRUCES.............J. L. Wilson
CUETO.............C. E. W. Ward

CUBA (Continued)

FLORIDA.............Z. Mederos
GUANTANAMO.........R. E. Symes
HAVANA..........{R. de Arozarena, Joint Mgr. / F.W. Bain, Joint Mgr. / F. Mejer, Asst. Mgr. / J.Fernandez Asst.Mgr.
GALIANO...........P. Carol
MONTE............F. Solozabal
MURALLA.........P. Suarez
VEDADO...........E. Acosta
JATIBONICO..........M. L. Brown
LA MAYA............C. Macias
MANZANILLO........M. Rubio

[65]

WEST INDIES (Continued)

CUBA (Continued)

MATANZAS..........A. Amoedo
MORON..............J. M. Fraser
NUEVITAS...........R. Yaguez
PALMA SORIANO......M. C. Fabre
PINAR DEL RIO......R. Prieto
PUERTO PADRE.......D. Aguero
SAGUA LA GRANDE.....G. Saenz
SANCTI SPIRITUS.....L. F. Canizares
SANTA CLARA........J. J. Gonzalez
SANTIAGO DE CUBA... {R. N. Herman / C. Arias, Assistant / J. G. Pulles, Assistant

PORTO RICO

MAYAGUEZ...........E. Bazan
PONCE..............L. A. Albizu
SAN JUAN.......... {R. G. Allen / W. H. Biscombe, Asst.

DOMINICAN REPUBLIC

PUERTO PLATA.........W. C. Reid
SANCHEZ..............L. J. McCarthy
SAN PEDRO DE MACORIS {J. Moll / A. L. J. Melanson, Assistant
SANTIAGO DE LOS CABALLEROS.........T. J. Reardon
SANTO DOMINGO....... {T. B. O'Connell / W. L. Smith, Asst.

HAITI

PORT-AU-PRINCE...... {W. A. Clark / A. J. Brandt, Asst.

GUADELOUPE

BASSE TERRE...........R. H. Goulet
POINTE-A-PITRE.........R. F. Leavitt

MARTINIQUE

FORT DE FRANCE........H. L. Gagnon

BRITISH WEST INDIES

ANTIGUA

ST. JOHN'S............W. H. Badley, Acting

BAHAMAS

NASSAU..............G. H. Gamblin

BARBADOS

BRIDGETOWN.........M. White, Acting
SPEIGHTSTOWN........H. L. Grant, Sub.

DOMINICA

ROSEAU..............S. Sands

GRENADA

ST. GEORGE'S.........A. H. Brebner

JAMAICA

KINGSTON.............H. H. Troop

MONTSERRAT

PLYMOUTH.............A. Bonyun

NEVIS

CHARLESTOWN.........A. Gioannetti, Sub.

ST. KITTS

BASSETERRE...........W. S. Jones

TOBAGO

SCARBOROUGH.........L. R. Melville

TRINIDAD

PORT OF SPAIN.........T. H. Dalgliesh
SAN FERNANDO........J. C. Weir

E. F. B. Johnston, K.C.
2nd Vice-President 1912-1919

W. J. Sheppard
Director since 1912

C. S. Wilcox
Director since 1912

F. Pigment
Director since 1912

WEST INDIES (Continued)

CUBA (Continued)

MATANZAS	L. Amoedo
MORON	J. M. Fraser
NUEVITAS	R. Yaguez
PALMA SORIANO	M. C. Fabre
PINAR DEL RIO	R. Prieto
PUERTO PADRE	D. Aguero
SAGUA LA GRANDE	G. Saez
SANCTI SPIRITUS	L. F. Cabrera
SANTA CLARA	J. J. Gonzalez
	R. N. Horton
SANTIAGO DE CUBA	C. Azar, Assistant
	J. Salleo, Assistant

PORTO RICO

MAYAGUEZ	T. Bean
PONCE	L. A. Albizu
SAN JUAN	R. G. Allen
	W. H. Biscombe, Asst.

DOMINICAN REPUBLIC

PUERTO PLATA	W. C. Reid
SANCHEZ	L. J. McCarthy
SAN PEDRO DE MACORIS	J. Moll
	A. L. J. Melanson, Assistant
SANTIAGO DE LOS CABALLEROS	T. J. Reardon
SANTO DOMINGO	T. B. O'Connell
	W. L. Smith, Asst.

HAITI

PORT-AU-PRINCE	W. A. Clark
	A. J. Brandt, Asst.

GUADELOUPE

BASSE TERRE	R. H. Goulet
POINTE-A-PITRE	R. F. Leavitt

MARTINIQUE

FORT DE FRANCE	H. L. Gagnon

BRITISH WEST INDIES

ANTIGUA

ST. JOHN'S............W. H. Badley, Acting

BAHAMAS

NASSAU ....G. H. Gamblin

BARBADOS

BRIDGETOWN.........M. White, Acting
SPEIGHTSTOWN........H. L. Grant, Sub.

DOMINICA

ROSEAU..............S. Sands

GRENADA

ST. GEORGE'S.... A. H. Brebner

JAMAICA

KINGSTON.............H. H. Troop

MONTSERRAT

PLYMOUTH.............A. Bonyun

NEVIS

CHARLESTOWN..........A. Gioannetti, Sub.

ST. KITTS

BASSETERRE............W. S. Jones

TOBAGO

SCARBOROUGH..........L. R. Melville

TRINIDAD

PORT OF SPAIN..........T. H. Dalgliesh
SAN FERNANDO...... J. C. Weir

[105]

E.F.B.Johnston,K.C.
2ⁿᵈ Vice-President 1912-1919

W.J.Sheppard
Director since 1912

C.S.Wilcox
Director since 1912

A.E.Dyment
Director since 1912

THE ROYAL BANK OF CANADA

CENTRAL AND SOUTH AMERICA

ARGENTINE

BUENOS AIRES....... {T. F. Dever
J. S. Nicholls, Asst.

BRAZIL

RIO DE JANEIRO...... {G. V. Long
W. C. Lowry, Asst.

URUGUAY

MONTEVIDEO.........R. G. Allen

VENEZUELA

CARACAS............Wm. Burns
CIUDAD BOLIVAR......H. P. Urich

VENEZUELA (Continued)

MARACAIBO.........A. D. Macgillivray
PUERTO CABELLO.....M. A. Schon

BRITISH GUIANA

GEORGETOWN.........Leon Colvin
NEW AMSTERDAM.....C. H. Bagot
ROSE HALL
(CORENTYNE).......N. G. Hohenkerk

BRITISH HONDURAS

BELIZE.............C. R. Beattie

COSTA RICA

SAN JOSÉ...........H. Watson

SPAIN

BARCELONA, PLAZA DE CATALUNA 6.....................C. E. Mackenzie, P. F. Smith, Asst.

UNITED STATES

NEW YORK, 68 WILLIAM ST.................. {F. T. Walker, Agent; J. A. Beatson, Agent;
E. B. McInerney, Agent; J. D. Leavitt, Agent

GREAT BRITAIN

LONDON, BANK BLDGS, PRINCES ST., E.C..............T. R. Whitley; J. Mackie, Joint Mgr.

AUXILIARY IN FRANCE

THE ROYAL BANK OF CANADA (FRANCE)
PARIS, 28 RUE DU QUATRE-SEPTEMBRE ....W. Warren; N. G. Hart, Assistant

ROLL OF HONOUR
MEMBERS OF THE STAFF WHO ENLISTED
FOR ACTIVE SERVICE
1914-1919

MEMBERS OF THE STAFF OF
THE ROYAL BANK OF CANADA
KILLED IN ACTION OR DIED OF WOUNDS

EDWARD JOHN ADDERLEY
WALTER GEORGE ADDISON
LESLIE FRANCIS ANTHONY
JOHN D'AUVERGNE HARRIS
ARUNDELL
JOHN WILLIAM AULDJO
GEORGE ALAN AUSTEN
CHARLES STUART BAILEY
KENNEDY GIDEON FRANCIS
BALDWIN
HERBERT DALLING BARLEE
SHEPPARD JAMES BARWIS
GEORGE JOHN MERCIER BATE
ROBERT SEDGEWICK BAYNE
ERROL STEWART BELL
ARTHUR FRED BELYEA
CARL AUGUST BENDER
ALFRED FITZHARDINGE MURRAY
BERKELEY
GEORGE MORTON BIRD
HARRY GODWIN DECIMUS BIRD
JAMES SOMERVILLE BLACK
WILLIAM BLACK
FREDERICK GEORGE BOLTON
DAVID CAMPBELL BRADSHAW
GEORGE MILLER BRIDEN
STANLEY VICTOR BRITTAN
DONALD DOUGLAS BROOKS
DONALD ARCHIBALD BROWN
HAROLD BROWN
WILFRED AUSTIN TORRANCE
BRYCE

JAMES AMBROSE CAIRNS
THOMAS CARGILL
THOMAS JOHNSTON CARSON
GEORGE RODERICK CHISHOLM, JR.
JOHN WALTER CHISHOLM
CLARENCE EDMUND COATES
ARTHUR HAMMOND COLE
THOMAS PEARSON COPP
GEORGE LORING CRAIG
CLAUDE HAROLD CROSS
JOHN HAROLD DEANS
JACQUES VALLETON DE BOIS-
SIERE
JOHN JOSEPH DELANEY
PAUL JEAN DESTRUBE
JOHN JAMES DOBLE
JAMES A. DOUGLAS
ANDREW THOMAS DOW
NELSON PATRICK DOYLE
JOHN RUTHERFORD DUFF
JOSEPH CLYNCH CAMPBELL
DUNCAN
WILLIAM ARTHUR PEEL DURIE
CHARLES CLEVELAND EASTLAND
JOHN FRANCIS EDENS
FRED FLETCHER ELLIOTT
CHARLES WESLEY ELSDON
DAVID THORNTON EMBREE
RICHARD ALBERT ESTEY
ARCHIBALD MCKENZIE FERGU-
SON
HERBERT FORBES

W. H. Thorpe
Director since 1907

William Robertson
Director 1910-1919

A. Woodward
Director since 1917

John T. Ross
Director since 1917

KILLED IN ACTION OR DIED OF WOUNDS (*Continued*)

Donald Drummond Fraser
Edward James Fright
William Gillies
John Glass
William Gardner Goldsworth
Thomas Goodsir
Kenneth Marshall Grant
David Clark Grieve
Leslie Alvin Gutteridge
John Horne Hamilton
WilliamRobertson Hamilton
Harold McDougall Hannah
Goldwin William Harron
Gordon Thomas Haszard
Arthur Wellesley Hatfield
Gerald Coussmaker Heath
Charles Hereron
Charles Hamilton Hobkirk
John Hodkinson
Cecil Sanford Holliday
James Swirles Hood
Roy Cameron Hunter
Wilfred Laurier Hunter
Arthur Andrew Hynes
Asgeir Johnson
Frank Lawrence Johnson
Mark St. Clair Johnston
Henry William Jones
John Hempenstall Kearney
John Joshua Wallace King
Charles Frederick Kirkman
Frederick Sylvester Kirvan
Alexander Rollo Laing
Lloyd Haliburton Langille
James Gordon Laurie

Eric Gilbert Leake
Alfred Johnson Leeming
Robert Winfield Lister
Ernest Victor Loney
Alexander Muir Lyon
Norman Stewart MacDonald
Arthur Gordon Mackay
Colin Gordon MacNaughton
Cyril Frederic Mann
Joseph Stanley McCoy
Harry Alexander McDonald
William Patrick McGibbon
GeorgeValentine McInerney
Lorne Howson McIntyre
Kenneth Wetzlar McLea
John McWilliam
Frederick Gerald Merritt
James Noble Layton Millett
Arthur Mitchell
Douglas Norman Moir
Hugh Boyd Montgomery
Cyril George Ettrick Moore
James Walker Moore
Donald Spence Morrison
James Maclaren Morton
Duncan MacNicoll Muir
Archie Bremner Nelson
James Albert Noble
Alfred Lloyd Norman
Charles Edward Pattison
Victor Reginald Pauline
Ralph Pelluet
Arthur Walker Peters
Allan Phillips
Richard Bramwell Pickering
Raymond Pigg

KILLED IN ACTION OR DIED OF WOUNDS (Continued)

WILLIAM ROSS PRINGLE
JAMES ALFRED RALSTON
JAMES MONILAWS RICHARDSON
JAMES HENRY RICHES
WILLIAM PATRICK ROSS
NORMAN HORACE PEMBERTON
  SALUSBURY
STEPHEN WILLIAM SCOTT
SYDNEY GEORGE SELLERS ·
FREDERICK HENRY SHARP
HERBERT VICTOR SHARPE
THOMAS PITCAIRN SHEARER
LAURENCE SHUSTER SHERMAN
DONALD DEVERE SHIELDS
JOHN ARTHUR MURTON SHORE
JOHN THOMSON SMITH
RALPH HENNIKER SMITH
TRENHOLME VASEY GOLDWIN
  SMITH
FENNELL ANDERSON SMYTH
FREDERICK WILLIAM SNOW
JOHNSTON LAWRENCE SNOWDON
RALPH ERSKINE SPENCE
JAMES HENDRY STEELE
CHARLES DISNEY PENDER
  STEIN

CHARLES NORIE STEPHEN
CLAUDE CASTLEMAINE TEMPLE
CHARLES GORDON THOMPSON
FRANK THORSTEINSON
HAMILTON SYLVESTER TAYLOR
  TILLEY
ROY ELSWORTH TOWER
DAVID MACKEGGIE TUACH
MURRAY LAMONT TUPPER
GEORGE ARCHER TURNBULL
WALTER JAMES TURNBULL
GEORGE WHITEFORD VAN
  KLEEK
CHARLES RICHMOND VOELKER
CHARLES WALKER WALLACE
HALIBURTON WALLACE
IVAN NEWELL WALLIS
GERALD EDWIN WELLS
CHURCHILL FREEMAN WEST
ARTHUR JENNINGS WILLIAMS
JAMES CARL WILLIAMSON
GEORGE THOMAS WILSON
RONALD JOHN WISHART
CECIL GEORGE WYATT

DIED IN HOSPITAL

STANLEY DUNCAN BOLE
JAMES KENNETH BUTLER
ALLISON HOOD FARNELL
VICTOR MIDDLETON HANNA
LOUIS KERR
DONALD MACPHAIL MAC-
  CALLUM

BYRON MURRAY
NORMAN MURRAY
WILLIAM NAIRN
WILLIAM HARDY NICHOLLS
JOHN MURRAY SKEAFF
REGINALD BAYLY WHITE
ESDON MELVILLE WOLFE

ROLL OF HONOUR

LIST OF 1,493 MEMBERS OF THE STAFF WHO ENLISTED FOR ACTIVE SERVICE, 1914-1919

. .

CASUALTIES		DECORATIONS	
Killed in Action or Died in Hospital ..	186	Distinguished Service Order.........	2
Wounded	119	Distinguished Service Cross	1
Missing......................	5	Military Cross...................	19
Prisoners of War.................	10	Bar to M.C.....................	3
	—	Distinguished Flying Cross	1
	320	Distinguished Conduct Medal	4
		Military Medal	16
		Bar to M.M.....................	1
			—
			47

✦ Killed in Action or Died of Wounds   ‡ Wounded   § Missing   * Was Prisoner of War

NAME	RANK	UNIT
*ABBEY, R.	Corporal . . .	4th C.M.R.
ABREU, R. C.	2nd Class Seaman	U.S. Coast Defence
ACKERMAN, W. W. D. . . .	Gunner	Div. Amm. Column
ACKLAND, W. A.	Sergeant	143rd Battn.
ACTON, HENRY	Lieutenant . . .	10th South Staffordshire Regt.
ADAMS, L. R.	Private	36th Battn.
ADAMS, P. H.	Private	147th Battn.
✦ADDERLEY, E. J.		
✦ADDISON, W. G. . .ʼ. . . .	Corporal . . .	3rd Div. Amm. Column
AINGER, F. W.	Cadet	Royal Air Force
AITCHISON, D.	Private	Wiltshire Regiment
AITKEN, J. M.	Captain	208th Battn.
AITKEN, W. S..	Gunner	C.F.A.
ALEXANDER, G. A.		61st Battn.
ALEXANDER, W. H. B. . . .		
ALLAN, E. I. R.	Gunner	R.C.H.A.
ALLEN, C. S.	Gunner	22nd C.F.A.
ALLEN, J. H. . . . : . . .	.Private	1st Depot Battn., Regina
ALLINGHAM, N. C.	Gunner	69th C.F.A.
ALLINGHAM, W. A.	Gunner	69th C.F.A.
ALLMAN, A. C.	Qmr.-Sergt. . .	159th Battn.
ALLMAN, E. J.	Flight Sergt. . .	Royal Air Force

[77]

NAME	RANK	UNIT
ALMOND, A. E.	Private	54th Battn.
‡AMSKOLD, E. C.	Private	347th M. G. Battn., Amer. Exp. Force
‡ANDERSON, A. D.	Sergeant	London Scottish
ANDERSON, J. T.	Trooper	34th Fort Garry Horse
ANDERSON, M.	Gunner	23rd C.F.A.
ANDERSON, R.	Private	43rd Battn.
ANDREW, M.	Private	R.N.W.M.P.
ANDREWES, F. L.	Private	24th Draft, Canadian Railway Troops.
ANDREWS, L. R.	2nd Lieutenant	5th Cont. B.W.I. Regt.
‡ANNAND, C. D.	Private	85th Battn.
+ANTHONY, L. F.	Lance-Corporal	25th Battn.
APPEL, V. E.	Mechanic	Royal Air Force
ARMBRISTER, C. (M.C. AND M.M.)	Lieutenant	54th Battn.
ARMSTRONG, F. C.	Lance-Corporal	23rd Res. Battn.
ARMSTRONG, N. H.	Gunner	67th C.F.A.
ARSENEAU, G. C.	Drummer	187th Battn.
+ARUNDELL, J. d'A. H.	Sergeant	14th Battn.
‡ATKIN, I. C. R. (M.C. AND BAR)	Captain	131st Battn.
ATKINS, B. M.		
ATKINSON, C. H.	Sergeant	40th Battn.
ATKINSON, T. H. (M.C.)	Captain	8th C.F.A.
AUCOIN, J. D.	Private	No. 3 Nova Scotia Forestry
AUDETTE, L. J.	Private	2nd Montreal Depot Battn.
+AULDJO, J. W.	Private	60th Battn.
+AUSTEN, G. A.	2nd Lieutenant	Divisional Cycle Corps
BADLEY, F. A.	Cadet	Royal Air Force
BAGOT, A. G.	Rifleman	6th Battn. London Regt.
+BAILEY, C. S.	Lieutenant	44th Battn.
BAILEY, S. McA.	Gunner	8th Siege Battery
BAINES, T.		
BAIRD, J.	Lance-Corporal	60th Battn.
BAIRD, J. D.	Corporal	5th Pioneer Battn.
BAIRD, J. W.	Gunner	68th C.F.A.
BAKER, A. D.	Signaller	Howitzer Battery, 8th Brigade C.F.A.

G. G. Stuart, K.C.
Director 1917 - 1918

W. H. McWilliams
Director since 1918

Capt. Wm. Robinson
Director since 1919

J. McTavish Campbell
Director since 1919

A. McTavish Campbell
Director since 1919

NAME	RANK	UNIT
BAKER, C. E.	Sergeant	216th Battn.
♦BALDWIN, K. G. F.	Corporal	6th C.M.R.
BALFOUR, R. H.	Lieutenant	R.A.F.
BALL, E. C.	Driver	71st C.F.A.
BALMAIN, D. H. (M.C.)	Captain	5th Canadian Engineers
BANKS, C. N.	Lance-Corporal	85th Battn.
BAPTIST, K. O.	Gunner	16th C.F.A.
BARIL, J. T.		
BARKER, H. G.	Sapper	6th Field Co., Can. Engineers
♦BARLEE, H. D.	Private	196th Battn.
BARLOW, D. S.	Driver	68th C.F.A.
BARNES, C. G. (D.C.M.)	Private	61st Battn.
BARNES, J. C.	Gunner	R.C.H.A.
BARNES, K. S.	Lieutenant	39th Can. Forestry Co.
BARR, W. M.	Sergeant	86th Battn.
BARRETT, R. P.		
BARRIE, C. G.	Cadet	Royal Flying Corps
BARRY, J. R.	Private	85th Battn.
BARTLETT, H. A.		
BARTON, W. R.	Lieutenant	75th Battn.
♦BARWIS, S. J.	Private	143rd Battn.
BATCHELOR, A. T.	Private	172nd Battn.
♦BATE, G. J. M.	Gunner	8th C.F.A.
‡BAXTER, J. (M.C.)	Captain	47th Battn.
BAXTER, J. McI.		
BAYER, R. O.	Gunner	8th Army Brigade, C.F.A.
BAYNE, E.		R.N.W.M.P.
‡BAYNE, E. G.		
♦BAYNE, R. S.		
BEAVAN, A. C.		
BEBBINGTON, W. T.	Lance-Corporal	32nd Battn.
BECKER, C. J.		
BEESTON, E. H.	Gunner	11th Can. Siege Artillery
BELISLE, J. W.	Cadet	Royal Air Force
‡BELL, E. R.	Staff-Sergt.	62nd Battn.
♦BELL, E. S.	Private	P.P.C.L.I.
BELL, J. E.	Lieutenant	124th Battn.
BELL, W. N.	Cadet	Royal Air Force

NAME	RANK	UNIT
BELLAIRS, B. A.	Private	R.A.S.C.
✝BELYEA, A. F.	Cadet	Royal Flying Corps
✝BENDER, C. A.	Cadet	Royal Flying Corps
BENDIKSEN, D.	Private	49th Battn.
BENSON, L. A.	Cadet	Royal Flying Corps
‡BENSON, P. R.	Private	28th Battn.
✝BERKELEY, A. F. M.		
BERWICK, H. B.	Private	R.A.F.
BESSEY, A. L.	Corporal	1st Canadian Field Ambulance
BETT, D. J.	Private	47th Battn.
BETT, G. W.	Staff-Sergeant	47th Battn.
BIBLE, C. H.	Private	19th Battn.
‡BICKERTON, J.	Private	3rd Battn.
BILODEAU, E.	Cadet	Royal Flying Corps
✝BIRD, G. M.	Private	62nd Battn.
✝BIRD, H. G. D.	Private	5th Battn.
BIRD, H. J.	Private	196th Battn.
BJORKLUND, S. J.		
BJORNSON, O. G	Private	C.A.P.C.
‡BLACK, A.	Private	P.P.C.L.I.
BLACK, J. D. K.	Gunner	64th C.F.A.
✝BLACK, J. S.	Private	46th Battn.
BLACK, O. C. E.		
BLACK, S. C.	Sergeant-Major	2nd Howitzer Battery, C.F.A.
✝BLACK, W.	Private	231st Battn.
BLAGRAVE, G. L.	Cadet	Royal Flying Corps
BLAIR, R. G.	Sergeant	25th Battn.
BLAKE, H. A. (M. C.)	Captain	4th C.M.R.
BLAKE, L. L.	Gunner	No. 5 Co., R.C.G.A.
BLANCHARD, H. L.	Private	1st D.B., 2nd C.O.R.
BLANCHFIELD, F. J.	Gunner	64th C.F.A.
BLENKINSOP, A.	Private	184th Battn.
BLOIS, R. E.	Private	2nd Depot Battn., Vancouver
BOLDUC, G.	Private	53rd C.F.A.
✝BOLE, S. D.	Trooper	Strathcona Horse
✝BOLTON, F. G.	Gunner	27th C.F.A.
‡BORLAND, D. C. G.	Private	46th Battn.
BORTHWICK, R. W.	Private	Saskatchewan Depot Battn.

[82]

R. Mac D. Paterson
Director since 1917

Robert Adair
Director since 1919

James Redmond
Director since 1905

R.Mac D.Paterson
Director since 1917

Robert Adair
Director since 1919

James Redmond
Director since 1906

NAME	RANK	UNIT
BOSIEN, D. E.	Cadet	Royal Air Force
BOSWELL, E. C.	Sub-Lieutenant	Motor Boat Patrol Service
BOUDREAU, A. T.	Private	1st Depot Battn., N.B. Regt.
BOUDREAU, J. E.	Cadet	Royal Air Force
BOUDREAU, L. P.	Sapper	Canadian Engineers
BOULANGER, J. H.	Cadet	Royal Air Force
BOURGEOIS, D.	Private	1st Depot Battn., Quebec
BOURQUE, L. J.	Private	1st Depot Battn., N.B. Regt.
BOVEL-JONES, L. C.	Trooper	Royal Can. Dragoons
BOWDEN, H. G.	Corporal	1st Newfoundland Regt.
‡BOWERS, C. C.	Lieutenant	R.A.F.
BOWSER, G.	Private	2nd Depot Battn., Victoria
BOYCE, E. W.		
BOYD, A. E.	Private	102nd Battn.
‡BOYD, G. A.	Corporal	23rd Reserve Battn.
‡BOYD, J.	Corporal	10th Battn.
BOYD, J. G. (M.M.)	Corporal	1st Can. D.A.C.
BOYD, R. J.	Private	85th Battn.
BRADLEY, E. R.	2nd Lieutenant	Royal Naval Air Service
‡BRADLEY, P. E.	Private	29th Battn.
✦BRADSHAW, D. C.	Q.-Master-Sergt.	37th Battn.
BRADWELL, W.		Can. Railway Troops
‡BRAIDWOOD, T.	Private	C.A.M.C.
BRAY, A. M.	Private	195th Battn.
BREESE, A. E. S.	Private	44th Battn.
§BREHON, R. C.		
BRENNEN, A. J.	Corporal	4th C.M.R.
BREWER, E. O.	Sergeant	104th Battn.
BREWSTER, G.	Sergeant	61st Battn.
✦BRIDEN, G. M.		
✦BRITTAN, S. V.	Lieutenant	13th Battn.
BROCKIE, J. D.	Private	Wiltshire Regt.
✦BROOKS, D. D.	Private	1st Can. Motor Machine Gun Brigade
BROOKS, H. R.	Lieutenant	R.N.V.R.
BROTHERTON, W. T.	Private	C.A.M.C.
✦BROWN, D. A.	Private	10th Battn.
BROWN, F. M.	Private	1st Depot Battn., E.O.R.

NAME	RANK	UNIT
BROWN, GUY B.		
♣BROWN, H.	Private	. . . . 3rd Battn.
BROWN, H. H.	Gunner	. . . . 64th C.E.F.
BROWN, M. G.	Private	. . . . 203rd Battn.
BROWN, R. C.		
BROWNE, A. H.		
BROWNE, A. S.	Private	. . . . No. 1 Nova Scotia Forestry
BROWNE, A. W. G.		
BROWNLOW, E. J.	Private	. . . . Can. Motor Machine Gun Section
BRUM, S. M.	Private	. . . . 1st Depot Battn., E.O.R.
BRUUN, A. G.	Cadet	. . . . Royal Air Force
♣BRYCE, W. A. T.	Gunner	. . . . 55th C.F.A.
‡BRYDEN, W. F. (M.C.AND BAR)	Lieutenant	. . . 8th Battn. South Lancs. Regt.
BRYSON, A. M.	Private	. . . . P.P.C.L.I.
BRYSON, W. E.	Private	. . . . 10th Siege Battery
BUCKLEY, W. A.	Stretcher-Bearer	185th Battn.
BUNTAIN, G. H.		Royal Flying Corps
BURCHARD, H. K.	Gunner	. . . . 98th Siege Battery
BURNS, M. V.	Private	. . . . 1st Depot Battn., Regina
*BURNS, R.	Trooper	. . . . 8th C.M.R.
BURNSIDE, B.	Cadet	. . . . Royal Air Force
BURR, E. H.	Lieutenant	. . . East Lancashire Regt.
BURROWS, F. R.		
BURROWS, N. R.	Major	. . . . . 169th Battn.
BURT, H. A.	Cadet	. . . . Royal Air Force
♣BUTLER, J. K.	Private	. . . . 25th Battn.
§BUTLER, J. W.	Lieutenant	. . . Imperial Forces
BUTTERFIELD, R. D.		
BYNOE, E. D.		
CAHILL, J. J.	Private	. . . . 5th Infantry Replacement Regt.
CAIN, C. L.	Private	. . . . 26th Can. Reserve Battn.
♣CAIRNS, J. A.	Lance-Corporal	. 105th Battn.
CAIRNS, W. J.	Gunner	. . . . 21st C.F.A.
CALDECOTT, G.	Sergeant	. . . .
CALDER, F. G.	Cadet	. . . . Royal Flying Corps

NAME	RANK	UNIT
CAMERON, A. W..		Royal Flying Corps
CAMERON, A. W. H.	Lieutenant	Royal Flying Corps
‡CAMERON, H. L.		
CAMERON, RANDOLPH	Sergeant	16th Battn.
CAMERON, S. K.		Royal Flying Corps
CAMIRAND, H.	Private	230th Battn.
‡CAMPBELL, H.	Private	72nd Seaforth Highlanders
CAMPBELL, J. ALEX.	Trooper	6th C.M.R.
CAMPBELL, J. ARTHUR	Gunner	36th C.F.A.
CAMPBELL, M..	Sergeant	231st Battn.
CAMPBELL, N. J..		
CAMPBELL, R. B.	Gunner	36th Howitzer Battery, C.F.A.
CAMPBELL, V. F.	Trooper	13th C.M.R.
CAMPBELL, W..	Private	B.C. Cyclist Platoon
CANFIELD, N. B.	Private	C.A.M.C.
CARD, C. W.	Private	1st Depot Battn., Calgary
✚CARGILL, T..	Private	6th Black Watch, B.E.F.
CARMICHAEL, J. V.		
✚CARSON, T. J.	Private	P.P.C.L.I.
CARSTAIRS, D. I..	Private	13th Battn.
CASSELS, C. L..	Private	134th Battn.
CASTRO, J. M.	Sergeant	373rd Infantry, U.S.A.
CASWELL, H. A.	Gunner	9th Infantry Brigade
CAWDRON, E. V.	Major	1st Ammunition Park
CHAMPAGNE, A. A.	Private	59th Battn.
CHAPIN, H. C..	Private	63rd C.F.A.
CHAPMAN, P. T.	Signaller	18th Battn.
CHARLTON, H. G.	Private	7th Battn.
CHATER, H. J.	Trooper	Strathcona Horse
CHATTERS, E. S.	Private	30th Battn.
CHILTON, A.	Captain	C.A.S.C.
CHINN, J. N.	Corporal	Div. Sig. Corps
CHISHOLM, A. D..	Private	C.A.M.C.
CHISHOLM, A. J.	Gunner	75th C.F.A.
✚CHISHOLM, JR., G. R.	Private	78th Battn.
CHISHOLM, J. D.	Sergeant	185th Battn.
✚*CHISHOLM, J. W..	Private	11th Battn.
CHOQUETTE, A. R.	Private	C.O.T.C., Laval

NAME	RANK	UNIT
CHRISTIAN, F. G.	Gunner	70th C.F.A.
CHRISTIE, K. G.	Gunner	2nd Div. Ammunition Col.
CLARK, B. W.	Acting Sergeant	13th Canadian Reserve Battn.
CLARK, E. J.	Private	49th Battn.
CLARK, H. F.	Conductor	Can. Ordnance Corps
CLARK, P. E.	Gunner	67th C.F.A.
CLARKE, H. H.	Private	248th Battn.
CLAY, P.	Gunner	68th C.F.A.
✦COATES, C. E.	Private	53rd Battn.
‡COATS, C.		
✦COLE, A. H.	Trooper	11th C.M.R.
‡COLE, D. H. (M.M.)	Lieutenant	27th C.F.A.
COLE, J. S.	Private	11th C.M.R.
COLE, R. J.	Gunner	67th C.F.A.
COLLETT, L.	Private	5th C.M.R.
COLVIN, W. D.		
COLWILL, C. W.	Gunner	72nd C.F.A.
CONNELLY, E. F.	Sapper	Canadian Engineers
CONNERY, P. H.	Private	218th Battn.
COOK, C. H.	Cadet	Royal Air Force
COOK, S. M.	Cadet	Royal Air Force
COOKE, C. L.	Staff-Sergt.	C.A.P.C.
COOMBES, W. J.	Private	27th Battn.
COOPER, G. A.	Gunner	72nd C.F.A.
COOPER, H. H.		
✦COPP, T. P.	Lieutenant	72nd Battn.
CORBETT, A. E.	Private	147th Battn.
CORBETT, D. R.	Sergeant	3rd Siege Battery, C.G.A.
CORBETT, E. E.	Private	Royal Air Force
CORBETT, R. O.		
CORNISH, H. H.	Flight Cadet	Royal Air Force
CORNWALL, H. A.	Sergeant	40th Battn.
COSMAN, E. A.	Private	Royal Canadian Regiment
COSTER, W. J.		
‡COTTER, J. G.	Private	185th Battn.
COTTRILL, J. D.	Gunner	64th C.F.A.
COULOMBE, J. E. I.	Private	6th Battery, R.C.G.A.
‡COUMANS, R. G.	Private	42nd Battn.

Original premises in Bedford Row, Halifax, occupied by "Merchants Bank"

Original premises in Bedford Row, Halifax, occupied by the "Merchants Bank"

NAME	RANK	UNIT
‡Courcier, R. C.		
Courtney, A. J.		
Coventry, J. H.	Private	1st Depot Battn.
Cox, A. J.		Royal Flying Corps
Cox, R. G.	Sergeant	Army Pay Corps
✦Craig, G. L.	Sergeant	236th Battn.
Craig, G. W.	Gunner	5th Siege Battery
Craig, W. A.	Private	102nd Battn.
‡Craig, W. E.	Signaller	27th C.F.A.
Crawford, C.	Private	P.P.C.L.I.
Crawford, F. W.	Gunner	63rd C.F.A.
Crawforth, M. S.	Gunner	70th C.F.A.
Creighton, H. R.	Gunner	67th C.F.A.
Creighton, S. D.	Private	Machine Gun Corps
‡Crocker, C. C.	Gunner	8th Battery, C.F.A.
Croil, D. R.	Gunner	3rd Siege Battery
Crooks, C. H.		
✦Cross, C. H.		
Cross, T. E.	Sergeant	19th County of London (Ter.)
Crowell, A. L.	Driver	5th Can. Div. Amm. Column
Crowell, C. L.	Private	85th Battn.
Cruickshank, L.	Lieutenant	4th Battn.
Cryer, S.		
Cullis, F. R.		
‡Cumming, A. (D.C.M.)	Sergeant	Canadian Infantry
‡Cumming, G.	Private	9th Battn.
Cummings, T. C.	Sapper	Canadian Engineers
‡Cunningham, H.	Private	40th Battn.
Cunningham, H. S. F.	Private	10th Battn., Can. G. Regt.
Curll, M. H.	Sergeant	85th Battn.
Currie, D. B.	Gunner	165th Siege Battery
Currie, G. C.	Sergeant	119th O. S. Battn.
Currie, T. D.	Captain	6th Can. Rly. Troops
Curtis, V. A.-St. C.	Gunner	9th Siege Battery
Curtis, W. A. (D.S.C.)	Flight Lieut.	Aviation Corps, R.N.A.S.
Cutten, C. B.	Gunner	7th Can. Siege Battery
‡Dale, F. S.	Lance-Corporal	1st C.M.R.
Daniel, G. H.	Private	C.A.M.C.

NAME	RANK	UNIT
DASHNEY, D. L.	Sergeant	5th Div. Amm. Column
DAVIDSON, L. K.	Lieutenant	R.A.F.
DAVIES, W. E.	Private	78th Battn.
DAVIES, W. J.	Gunner	10th Siege Battery
DAVIS, C. R.	Q.-Master-Sergt.	40th C.F.A.
DAVISON, B. A.		
DAVISON, H. A.	Gunner	107th Siege Battery
DAVISON, R.	Sergeant	Royal Air Force
DAVY, A. C.	2nd Lieutenant	Royal Fusiliers
DAWES, H. W.		
DAWSON, C. S.	Private	Royal Flying Corps
‡DAY, E. A.	Private	2nd Battn. 1st Nfld. Regt.
DAY, H. R.	Lieutenant	44th Battn.
DAYKIN, R. O.		Royal Flying Corps
DEAN, J. (M.M.)	Gunner	3rd C.D.A.C.
DEAN, R. H.	Lieutenant	26th Battn.
✦DEANS, J. H.	Lieutenant	Royal Flying Corps
‡DEAS, A. MacK	Private	3rd Battn.
✦DE BOISSIERE, J. V.	Lieutenant	4th Cont. B.W.I. Regt.
DE LA FONCHAIS, J.		
✦DELANEY, J. J.	Private	15th Battn.
DEMERS, J. C.	Sergeant	85th Battn.
DENTON, I. H.	Cadet	Royal Flying Corps
D'ENTREMONT, L. J.	Private	1st Depot Battalion
DESBRISAY, A. ST. C.	Trooper	6th C.M.R.
✦DESTRUBE, P. J.	Private	22nd Battn.
DEVERMANN, C. A.	Private	7th Regt., Company D.
‡DEVERTEUIL, M.	Trooper	King Edward's Horse
DE VERTEUIL, R. J.		Royal Air Force
DEVESON, B. L.		
DEVLIN, J. J.	Driver	C. Battery, R.C.H.A.
DEWAR, C. G.	Private	1st C.O.R.
DEWAR, J.	Corporal	104th Battn.
DE WOLF, A. W. (D.C.M.)	Lieutenant	3rd Siege Battery
DEXTER, R. S.	Private	1st Can. Cas. Station, B.E.F.
DICK, J. P.	Q.M.S.	31st Battn.
‡DICKIE, E. C.	Private	25th Battn.
DICKIE, K. R.	Private	10th Siege Battery

Halifax, N.S. Present Premises

Halifax, N. S. Present Premises

NAME	RANK	UNIT
‡Dickie, L. W.	Private	25th Battn.
Dickson, J. D.	Gunner	67th C.F.A.
Diespecker, E. J.	Bugler	48th Battn.
Diespecker, R. E. A.	Corporal	30th Battn.
Dillane, C. E. H.	Sapper	153rd Battn.
Dion, J. C. C.	Cadet	R.F.C.
‡Dixon, H. A.	Private	46th Battn.
‡Dobbin, C. E. B.	Lieutenant	97th Battn.
✦Doble, J. J.	Lieutenant	116th Battn.
Dodd, W. O.	2nd Class Mechanic	Royal Air Force
Dodge, C. M.	2nd Lieut.	R.G.A.
Dolan, M. G.	Private	1st Depot Battn., 1st C.O.R.
Donald, W. J.	Private	15th Reserve Battn.
Dooley, R. H.	Private	10th Canadians, B.E.F.
Doucette, H. H.	Private	112th Battn.
Dougherty, L. C.		
✦Douglas, J. A.		
Douse, G. A. P.	Lance-Corporal	42nd Battn.
‡Douse, H. B.	Private	21st Battn.
Dove, H. R.	Private	72nd Battn.
✦Dow, A. T.	Private	10th Battn.
Doyle, M. L. (d.f.c.)	Captain	199th Battn. (attached to Royal Flying Corps)
✦Doyle, N. P.	Private	91st Battn.
Drescher, J. V.	Private	1st Depot Battn., Regina
Dron, F.		
Drummond, W. W.		"D" Co., 10th Battn.
Dryden, A. S.	Sergeant	29th C.F.A.
✦Duff, J. R.	Private	P.P.C.L.I.
Duke, J. W.	Sapper	Royal Engineers
Dunbar, R. A. A.	Gunner	64th Battery, C.F.A.
Duncan, G. L.	Private	308th Regt., Field Artillery, U.S.A.
‡Duncan, G. T.	Private	1st Newfoundland Regt.
✦Duncan, J. C. C.	Private	13th Battn.
Duncan, W. B.		
Duncanson, R. T.	Private	49th Battn.

NAME	RANK	UNIT
Dunlop, F.		
Durham, E. B.	Gunner	7th Can. Siege Battery
✦Durie, W. A. P.	Lieutenant . . .	58th Battn.
Dustan, S. G.	Private	Div. Signalling Corps
Duval, O.	Private	2nd Quebec Regt.
Dymock, W. A.	Corporal . . .	C.A.S.C.
Eason, A. S.	Private	Base Co., 63rd Batt.
Easson, A. A.	Gunner	50th C.F.A.
East, C.	Private	67th C.F.A.
✦Eastland, C. C. (m.m.). . .	Private	187th Battn.
Eaves, F. E.	Private	P.P.C.L.I.
Eckel, N. R.	Bombardier . .	23rd C.F.A.
Eden, F. E.		Ship *Ypres*, Canadian Navy.
Edens, F. A.	2nd Lieutenant .	1st Newfoundland Regt.
✦Edens, J. F.	.Lieutenant . . .	1st Newfoundland Regt.
‡Edmondson, W. K. . . .	Private	49th Battn.
Edwards, E. E.	Private	59th Battn.
Eiler, L. St. C.	Sergeant	44th Battn.
Elleray, R. H.	Private	Royal Fusiliers
✦Elliott, F. F.	Lieutenant . . .	7th Battn.
Elliott, R. P.	Lieutenant . . .	R.F.A. .
Elliott, W. B.	Private	164th Battn.
Ellis, A. C.	Lance-Corporal .	15th Battn.
Ellsworth, E. S.		Royal Air Force
Elmer, H. W.	Private	20th Battn.
Elmer, S. G.		
✦Elsdon, C. W.	Gunner	7th C.F.A.
✦Embree, D. T.	Sergeant	58th Battn.
Emerson, E. L.	Cadet	Royal Flying Corps
Emmett, R. E.		
Ernst, W. A.	Gunner	10th Halifax Siege Battery
✦Estey, R. A.	Private	25th Battn.
Evelyn, A. F.	2nd Lieut. . . .	4th London Regt.
Eykelbosch, C.	Private	195th Battn.
‡Eyre, Vincent		
Fairles, C. E.	Private	1st Canadian Tank Battn., C.M.G.C.

NAME	RANK	UNIT
Farmer, J. E.	Gunner	67th Battery, C.F.A.
+Farnell, A. H.		6th C.M.R.
Farquharson, J.	Flight Cadet	R.A.F.
Farr, G. R.	Private	C.A.S.C.
‡Farrah, J. R.	Private	91st Battn.
Farrar, W. F. (m.c.)	Captain	Tank Corps
Farrell, W. D.	Private	72nd C.F.A.
Feeney, G. W.	Private	1st Can. Reserve Battn.
Fell, V. R. (m.m. and bar)	Sergeant	1st M.G. Battn. (and P.P.C.L.I.)
Fenwick, W. S.	Gunner	67th C.F.A.
Fergus, J.	2nd Lieutenant	43rd Battn.
+Ferguson, A. McK.	Private	C.A.S.C.
Ferguson, H. W.	Sergeant	C.A.M.C.
Ferguson, W. I.	Private	15th Battn.
Ferrill, Max B.	Private	312th Amm. Train
Fielding, A. L.	Private	1st Depot Battn., W. Ont. Regt.
Finlayson, A.	Private	153rd Batt.
Finlayson, J.	Private	C.A.M.C.
Finlayson, J. K.		
Fisher, J. H. (m.m.)	Private	68th Battn.
Fisher, J. P.	Gunner	68th C.F.A.
Fitzgerald, C. W. B.	Lieutenant	Connaught Rangers
Fitzgerald, G. M.	Lieutenant	129th Battn.
Fitzpatrick, C. E. J.	Private	153rd Battn.
Flannery, C. G.	Private	C.A.D.C.
Flannigan, J. R.	Private	196th Battn.
Flaten, A.		U. S. Navy
Fleck, A. I.	Sergeant	66th C.F.A., 14th Brigade
Fleming, W. L.	Private	Royal Canadian Dragoons
Fletcher, C. B.	Sergeant	109th Batt.
Flinn, G.	Corporal	219th Battn.
Flinn, G. G.	Lieutenant	10th Battn.
Foley, N. T.	Sapper	Canadian Engineers
Foote, F.	Private	210th Battn.
+Forbes, H.	Trooper	1st C.M.R.
Ford, W. N.	Private	1st Depot Battn., 2nd C.O.R.

NAME	RANK	UNIT
FORGET, J. E.	Corporal	2nd Quebec Regt.
FORSYTH, J. S. G.	Driver	3rd Div. Sig. Corps.
FOSTER, R. P. (M.C.)	Lieutenant	131st Battn.
FOTHERGILL, G. L.	Lance-Corporal	Headquarters, C.F.A., 9th Brigade
FOX, J. B.	Captain	R.A.F.
FOX, R. E.	Captain	138th Battn.
FRASER, A. M.	Lieutenant	40th Battn.
✦FRASER, D. D.	Sergeant	1st Battn.
FRASER, L. G.	Sergeant	10th Halifax Siege Battery
FREELAND, W.	Private	C.A.M.C.
FREEBORN, W. C.	Private	110th Battn.
✦FRIGHT, E. J.	Private	36th Battn.
FULLERTON, D. S. T.		
FURLONG, F. W.	Private	18th Can. M.G. Co.
FURLONG, J. M.	Private	208th Battn.
GABLE, F. A.		Royal Air Force
GAETZ, T. H.		
‡GAGE, L. G.	Private	C.P.T.D. (Signal Base)
GALE, R. H.	Captain	74th Battn.
GANT, F. J.	Gunner	78th C.F.A.
GARDNER, W.	Private	3rd Battn.
GARLAND, W. J.	Sergeant	43rd Battn.
‡GARNEAU, L. V. (M.M.)	Private	87th Battn.
‡GARRETT, R.	Private	3rd Machine Gun Depot
GASKILL, G.	Pay Sergeant	C.A.P.C.
GASKIN, D. C.	Gunner	107th Siege Battery
‡GASS, C.	Lance-Corporal	25th Battn.
GATELEY, B. T.		
GAYLOR, F. C.		
GAYTON, W. A.		
GERALD, F. D.	Private	C.A.S.C.
GERALD, G. A.	Lieutenant	109th Battn.
GERVAN, H. V.	Private	72nd Battn.
GIBBON, L. M.	Private	50th Battn.
GIBBS, C.	Private	231st Battn.
GIBSON, C. B.	Lieutenant	Royal Flying Corps

Toronto, Ont.

NAME	RANK	UNIT
Fozof , . E	Corporal . . .	2nd Quebec Regt.
Forsy u, J S. G.	Driver	3rd Div. Sig. Corps.
Fatti R. P. (M.C.)	Lieutenant . . .	131st Battn.
Forthgill, G. L.	Lance-Corporal .	Headquarters, C.F.A., 9th Brigade
Fox, J B.	Captain	R.A.F.
Fox, K E.	Captain	138th Battn.
Fraser, A. M.	Lieutenant . . .	40th Battn.
+Fraser, D. D. . . .	Sergeant	1st Battn.
Fraser, L. G. . . .	Sergeant	10th Halifax Siege Battery
Fraser, D W . . .	Private	C.A.M.C.
Ferguson W . .	Private	110th Battn.
Gun .	Private	36th Battn.
Gale in S T . . .	.	
Gauk , F W . . .	Private . . .	18th Can. M.G. Co.
Gracy J M	Private . . .	208th Battn.
Gable F A.		Royal Air Force
Gietz. I. H.		
Gage, L. G.	Private . . .	C.P.T.D. (Signal Base)
Gale, K. H	Captain . . .	74th Battn.
Gost, F. J.	Gunner . . .	78th C.F.A.
Gardner, W.	Private . . .	3rd Battn.
Garland, W. J.	Sergeant . . .	43rd Battn.
Gineau, L. V. (M.M.) . . .	Private . . .	87th Battn.
Garrett, R.	Private . . .	3rd Machine Gun Depot
Gaskell, G.	Pay Sergeant .	C.A.P.C.
Gaskin, D. C.	Gunner	107th Siege Battery
Gass, C.	Lance-Corporal .	25th Battn.
Gatley, B. T.		
Gatlon, F. C.		
Gayton W. A.		
Gerald, F D	Private	C.A.S.C.
Gibald A	Lieutenant . . .	109th Battn.
Gilman H. V	Private	72nd Battn.
Gibson, L. M	Private	50th Battn.
Gimb, ...	Private	231st Battn.
Gray C B.	Lieutenant . . .	Royal Flying Corps

[98]

Toronto, Ont.

NAME	RANK	UNIT
GILBERT, H. B.	Quartermaster	40th Battn.
GILCHRIST, R. M.	Private	4th Can. Pioneers
GILL, V. L. F.		
‡GILLEN, R. D.	Private	231st Battn.
+GILLIES, W.	Private	29th Battn.
GILLMAN, R. O'D.		
GILMER, F. J.	Private	75th Battn.
GILMOUR, M. H.	Sergeant	11th C.R.T.
‡GIRVAN, W. G.	Sergeant	236th Battn.
GISBY, J. S.	Sergeant	46th Battn.
GLASS, C. H.		Veterinary Corps
+GLASS, J.	Lance-Corporal	87th Battn.
GLEGG, W. A. B.	Gunner	9th Siege Battery
GLEN, W.	Private	C.A.M.C. 1st Ambulance
GLENCROSS, H. P.	Sergeant	104th Battn.
GODIN, J. R.	Private	1st Can. Field Ambulance
GOHL, R. W.	Clerk	Royal Flying Corps
GOLD, W. H.	Private	1st Depot Battn., Calgary
GOLDBERG, S.	Sergeant	49th Battn.
+GOLDSWORTH, W. G.	Private	79th C.F.A.
GOODDAY, E. C.	Sergeant	97th Battn.
+GOODSIR, T.	Private	16th Battn.
GOODWIN, C. I.		Royal Air Force
GORDON, E. D.		Naval Wireless Operators
GORDON, W. J.		
GORHAM, E. R.	Gunner	No. 9 Siege Battery
GOUDEY, K. H.	Sergeant	85th Battn.
GOULET, J. A. J.	Cadet	Royal Air Force
GOW, A. D.	Cadet	Royal Air Force
GRAHAM, AUBREY F.	Private	Canadian Engineers
‡GRAHAM, E. R.	Private	67th Battn.
GRAHAM, W. A.	Lieutenant	British West India Regt.
GRAHAM, W. K.	Gunner	64th C.F.A.
GRAINGER, J. H.	Private	228th Battn.
GRANT, B. E.	Gunner	28th C.F.A.
GRANT, D. N.		
+GRANT, K. M.	Sergeant	29th C.F.A.
GRAYDON, J. C.	Sergeant	26th Co., Can. Forestry Corps

NAME	RANK	UNIT
GREEN, C.	Private	1st Newfoundland Regt.
GREEN, J. R.	Private	55th Battn.
GREEN, W.	Private	Expeditionary Force for Siberia
GREENWOOD, S. B.	Private	43rd Battn.
GREGOR, J.	Gunner	79th C.F.A.
GREGORY, B. J.	Private	141st Battn.
GRENVILLE, J. R.	Sergeant	2nd Can. Div. Training Battn.
✦GRIEVE, D. C.	Lieutenant	13th Battn.
GRIFFIN, G. A.	Private	157th Battn.
GRIFFITH, E. J.	Captain	
GRIFFITHS, C.	Sapper	6th Canadian Engineers
GRONDINES, L. P.		
GRYLLS, S. A.	Private	1st Canadian Tank Battn.
GUDMUNDSON, H.		
GUNN, A. R. D.	Private	67th Battery C.F.A.
GUNN, C. V.		
✦GUTTERIDGE, L. A.	Private	62nd Battn.
HACHEY, J. E.	Private	8th Field Ambulance Corps
HAGERMAN, S. H.	Lieutenant	Royal Flying Corps
HAGERMAN, W. A.	Private	7th Can. Stat'y Hospital
HAINES, R. S.	Private	219th Battn.
HAINES, T. E.	Sergeant	P.P.C.L.I.
HALE, J. A.	Captain	Can. Army Pay Corps
HALL, H. L.	Gunner	10th Halifax Siege Battery
HALL, JAMES P.		
HALLAM, A. G.	Private	105th Battn.
HALLETT, JAMES		
HALLIDAY, R.	Private	78th Battn.
HAM, N. L.	Private	P.P.C.L.I.
HAMILTON, D. I.	Gunner	64th C.F.A.
HAMILTON, F. G. W.	Private	151st Battn.
✦HAMILTON, J. H.	Private	15th Battn.
HAMILTON, J. W.	Private	103rd Battn.
HAMILTON, W. E.	Captain	10th Battn.
✦HAMILTON, W. R.	Private	7th Battn.
‡HANDLING, R. D.	Private	72nd Battn.

NAME	RANK	UNIT
+HANNA, V. M.	Private	219th Battn.
+HANNAH, H. McD.	Corporal	194th Battn.
HANNAHSON, A. C.	Cadet	Royal Air Force
HARCOURT, W. V. T.	Gunner	2nd Can. Heavy Artillery
HARDING, H. W.	Private	7th Division Regt.(P.O. Dep.) U.S.A.
HARDING, W. O. F.		
HARPER, E.	2nd Aviation Mechanic	Royal Flying Corps
HARRIS, W. W.	Gunner	70th C.F.A.
+HARRON, G. W.		28th Battn.
HART, G. M.	Private	C.A.S.C.
HARVEY, J. G. M.	Private	C.A.M.C.
HARVEY, K. E.	Corporal	75th Battn.
HARVEY, R. N.	Lieutenant	Royal Air Force
HARWOOD, A. E.	Private	72nd Battn.
HASLAM, G. W.	Private	164th Battn.
HASSING, T. C.	Cadet	Royal Air Force
+HASZARD, G. T.	Gunner	C.A.S.C.
HATCH, R. D.	Private	Royal Flying Corps
+HATFIELD, A. W.	Lance-Sergeant	25th Battn.
HATFIELD, H.	Private	63rd Battn.
HAWKINS, G. S.		
HAY, D. J.	Lieutenant	16th Battn., Royal Fusiliers
HAY, G. M.	Gunner	63rd C.F.A.
HAYWARD, L. C.	Lance-Corporal	1st Newfoundland Regt.
+HEATH, G. C.		
HEBENTON, W.	Gunner	58th C.F.A.
HENDERSON, H. F.	Sapper	Canadian Engineers
‡HENDERSON, H. H.	Lieutenant	84th Battn.
HENDERSON, J. D.	Private	C.A.S.C.
HENDERSON, M.	Corporal	62nd Battn.
HENDRY, G.	Private	147th Battn.
HENRY, B. D.	Private	110th Battn.
HENRY, G. A. V.		
HENRY, J. (M.M.)	Sergeant	5th Div. C.F.A.
HENSTRIDGE, F. C. B.	Lance-Corporal	7th Can. Trench Mortar Bty.
‡HEPBURN, W. V.	Private	107th Battn.

NAME	RANK	UNIT
+HERERON, C. (M.M.)	Lieutenant	2nd C.M.R.
HERMAN, R. R.	Lieutenant	25th Battn.
HERON, HERBERT	Sergeant	5th Western Cavalry, U.S.A.
HESLER, H. G.	Driver	Div. Amm. Column
HEUGHAN, A. J.	Lance-Corporal	1st Reinforcement Co., R.H. of C.
HICKS, W. B.	Private	85th Battn.
HILL, A. S.	Sergeant	87th Battn.
HILL, B.	Private	28th Battn.
HILL, W. (M.M.)	Lieutenant	C.A.M.C.
‡HIPWELL, H. R.	Lieutenant	
HISCOTT, B. C.	Private	7th Battn.
HOBART, A. W.		R.A.F.
+HOBKIRK, C. H.	Lieutenant	64th Battn.
HODGES, E. H.	Gunner	67th C.F.A.
+HODKINSON, J.	Private	72nd Battn.
HODSMAN, J. E.		
HODSON, G. C. (D.S.O.)	Lieut.-Col.	Can. Infantry
HOGAN, CLIFFORD	Gunner	74th C.F.A.
HOGARTH, W.	Private	210th Battn.
HOGG, A. C.	Lieutenant	3rd Can. Div. Amm. Column
+HOLLIDAY, C. S.	Private	203rd Battn.
HOLLOWAY, T. D.	Gunner	73rd C.F.A.
HOLMES, C. H.	Gunner	78th C.F.A.
HOLMES, E. A.		R.A.F.
‡HOLT, JOHN		
HOLTBY, A. V. C.		Strathcona Horse
HOLTBY, D. W.	Private	232nd Battn.
‡HOLTBY, V.	Private	17th Can. Railway Troops
+HOOD, J. S.	Lieutenant	23rd Battn.
HOOKER, C. B.	Cadet	R.A.F.
HOOTEN, R. H.		
HOPSON, W. S.	Driver	64th Battery
HORNER, R. R.	Sergeant	112th Battn.
HOUGH, J.	Sergeant	196th Battn.
HOUSTON, W. D.	Lance-Corporal	C.A.S.C.
HOWE, F. H.	Signaller	21st C.F.A.
HOWEY, J. L.		

Ottawa, Ont.

Quebec, Que.

NAME	RANK	UNIT
HUGHES, E. W.	Private	First Tank Battn.
HUGHSON, E. B.	Cadet	R.F.C.
HUNT, C. H.	2nd A. M.	R.F.C.
HUNTER, G. D.	Gunner	75th Battery
HUNTER, H. G.	Sergeant	24th Battn.
+HUNTER, R. C.		
+HUNTER, W. L.	Private	12th Battn.
HURST, H. G.		
HUSTON, A. T.	Lieutenant	5th Co. N.Y. Div., U.S. Army
HUSTWICK, W.	Private	12th Battn.
+HYNES, A. A.	Private	37th Battn.
IRONS, R. B.	Cadet	Royal Air Force
IRIARTE, R.	2nd Lieut.	374th Infantry, U.S.A.
IRVINE, G. B.	Corporal	7th Battn.
IRWIN, J. K. (D.C.M.)	Sergt.-Major	38th Battn.
JACK, P. G.	Lieutenant	5th C.M.R.
JACKSON, J. M.	Lieutenant	C.A.S.C.
JACOBS, W. H.	Corporal	159th Battn.
JAFFRAY, H. W.	Private	Div. Cycle Corps
‡JAMES, C. H. J.	Lieutenant	12th Res. Squad., R.A.F.
JARRELL, J. L.	Private	184th Battn.
JARVIS, S. R.	Lieutenant	19th Battn.
JEFFERY, L. A.	Captain	B.W.I. Regt.
JESSAMINE, J. M.		
+JOHNSON, A.		
+JOHNSON, F. L.	Lieutenant	British West India Regt.
JOHNSON, J. B.	Private	102nd Battn.
JOHNSON, J. C.		Royal Air Force
JOHNSON, R. H.	Private	14th London Scottish
JOHNSTON, A.	Private	1st Depot Battn., E.O.R.
‡JOHNSTON, G. H.	Private	C.M.G.C.
JOHNSTON, H. A.	Captain	13th Battn.
(D.S.O. AND M.C.)		
JOHNSTON, J. L.	Qmr.-Sergt.	64th Battn.
+JOHNSTON, M. ST. C.	Private	129th Battn.
JOHNSTON, W. J.	Gunner	55th C.F.A.

Edmonton, Alta.

Winnipeg, Man.

NAME	RANK	UNIT
JOLLEY, J. A.	Lieutenant	205th Battn.
JONES, D. E.	Gunner	67th C.F.A.
✦JONES, H. W.	Private	30th Battn.
JONES, R. L.	Private	196th Battn.
JONES, T. C. M.		
JUPP, R. L.	Driver	40th C.F.A.
KAYE, J. F. B.	Lieutenant	Shropshire Regt.
‡KEABLE, E. R.	Corporal	19th County of London (Terr.)
✦KEARNEY, J. H.	Private	14th Battn.
KEAST, J. R.	Sergeant	36th C.F.A.
KEATLEY, G.	Private	54th Battn.
KELLY, M. M.	Private	8th Field Ambulance Corps
KEILY, R. H.	Lieutenant	180th Battn.
‡KIMBLE, A. F.	Lieutenant	Suffolk Regt.
‡§KEMPTON, J.		
KENNEDY, E. J. A.	Private	2nd Depot Batt., 2nd C.O.R.
KENNETT, A.	Lieutenant	C.F.A.
KENNETT, FRANK	Lieutenant	C.F.A.
KERR, C. S.	Private	58th Battn.
✦KERR, L.	Gunner	70th Overseas Battery
KETCHESON, C. W.	Cadet	R.A.F.
KETTLES, A. G.	2nd Lieutenant	R.F.C., 66th Squad., Italy
KIERSTEAD, A. L.	Sergeant	38th C.F.A.
KINAHAN, A. A.	Corporal	147th Battn.
KING, D. A.	Sergeant	40th Battn.
✦KING, J. J. W.	Private	64th Battn.
KINGSTON, F. G.	Private	C.A.S.C.
KINZIE, G. G.	Sapper	Can. Engineers
KIRK, G. C.	Gunner	76th C.F.A.
KIRK, J. H.	Lieutenant	Royal Flying Corps
✦KIRKMAN, C. F.	Private	31st Battn.
✦KIRVAN, F. S.	Signaller	160th Battn.
KJOSNESS, E. S.	Cadet	R.A.F.
KNOWLES, J. E.		
KRUEGER, H.	Gunner	70th C.F.A.
KYDD, M. S.	Gunner	68th Depot Field Battery, C.F.A.

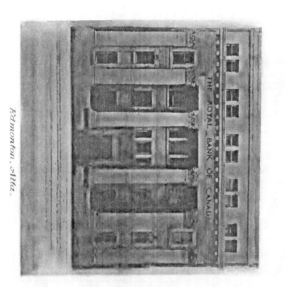

Edmonton, Alta.

Winnipeg, Man.

NAME	RANK	UNIT
Kyle, A. R.	Private	1st Quebec Regt.
Kynoch, A. E.	Corporal	2nd C.M.R.
Kyte, S. E.	Sergeant	40th Battn.
LaBonte, J. D.	Lieutenant	R.A.F.
✦Laing, A. R.	Private	47th Battn.
Lalande, H. J.	Private	Royal Canadian Infantry
Lally, W. L.	Seaman	U.S. Navy
L'Ami, C. E.	Private	183rd Battn.
L'Amie, W. G. C.		
‡Lamountain, Ernest	Bugler	60th Battn.
Lancefield, C. I.	Lieutenant	Royal Air Force
Landriau, W. F.	Gunner	5th Can. Div. Amm. Column
Lane, W. L.	Private	187th Battn.
✦Langille, L. H.	Private	219th Battn.
Langley, F. G.	Private	35th Battn.
Larson, L. R.		
Lauder, T. A.	Private	147th Battn.
Laurie, H. C.		
✦Laurie, J. G.	Captain	173rd Battn.
Lawlor, W. A.	Sapper	Can. Engineers
Lawson, J. M.		
Leach, L. H.	Gunner	72nd Battery
Leader, S.	Corporal	King Edward's Horse
✦Leake, E. G.	Lieutenant	7th Manchester Regt.
Leavitt, C. G.	Sergeant	No. 1 Depot Battn., N.S.
Leavitt, W. R.	Sergeant	26th Battn.
Leeder, J. J.	Private	156th Battn.
✦Leeming, A. J.	2nd Lieut.	Royal Fusiliers
‡Lees, H. A.	Private	7th Battn.
Lees, R. O.		
Lehman, A. J.	Private	York and Simcoe Foresters
Leiper, A.	Private	124th Battn.
LeLievre, P.	Private	1st Depot Battn. N.S. Regt.
Lemon, C. F.		
Lengfield, R. W.	Private	Can. Skilled R'y. Troops
Lennard, D.	Private	Middlesex Regt.
Leslie, A.	Private	1st Depot Battn., W.O.R.

NAME	RANK	UNIT
⸴ LESLIE, B. N.	Sapper	Canadian Engineers
LESLIE, W. L.	Private	202nd Battn.
LEWIS, D. J.		
LEWIS, P. G.	Cadet	R.F.C.
LEWIS, R. J.	Gunner	67th C.F.A.
LIND, C. E.	Lieutenant	R.F.C.
LINDSAY, M. A. F.	Private	26th Battn.
LINDSAY, R. T. K.	Private	C.A.S.C
LINTON, A. C. (M.C.)	Lieutenant	19th County of London (Terr.)
✦LISTER, R. W.	Private	14th Battn.
LITTLE, D. G.	Private	184th Battn.
LITTON, W.		
LIVINGSTON, H. S.	Cadet	R.F.C.
‡LOCKHART, D. P.	Private	72nd Battn.
⸴ ✦LONEY, E. V.	Corporal	194th Battn.
LONGLEY, E. G.	Gunner	10th Siege Battery
LORDLY, E. F.	Private	85th Battn.
LOUGHLEEN, H. L.	Private	C.A.M.C.
⸴ LOVE, H. A. (M.C.)	Captain	85th Battn.
LOVE, THOMAS	Lieutenant	C.A.S.C.
‡LOWE, G. S.	Private	65th Battn.
LOWE, L. W.	Private	2nd Depot Battn., E.O.R.
LOWRIE, J. H.	Captain	C.A.P.C.
LUCAS, S. J. (M.M.)	Private	52nd Battn.
‡LUMSDEN, S.		P.P.C.L.I.
‡LUMSDEN, W. W.	Lieutenant	67th Battn.
LUNNEY, G. D.	Private	147th Battn.
LYLE, J. N.	Gunner	44th C.F.A.
✦LYON, A. M.	Private	72nd Battn.
‡MACAULAY, W. G.	Sergeant	Royal Scots
✦MACCALLUM, D. MacP.	Private	77th Battn.
MACARTHUR, J. D.	Private	43rd Battn.
MACARTHUR, J. W.	Cadet	R.F.C.
MACASKILL, J.	Private	No. 3 General Hospital
MACDONALD, A. A.	Private	1st Pioneer Battn.
‡MACDONALD, A. J.	Lance-Corporal	5th Battn.
‡MACDONALD, A. R.	Captain	3rd Battn.

THE ROYAL BANK OF CANADA

NAME	RANK	UNIT
MacDonald, D. A.	Lance-Corporal	49th Battn.
Macdonald, D. W.	Private	Can. Engineers
MacDonald, G. C.	Driver	40th C.F.A.
Macdonald, H. C.	Private	68th Battery C.F.A.
Macdonald, J. P.	Sub-Lieutenant	R.F.C.
✚MacDonald, N. S.		
Macdonald, R. A.	Gunner	27th Battery, C.F.A.
MacDougall, E. D.	Private	52nd Battn.
MacDougall, J. L.	Private	40th Battn.
MacDougall, R.	Captain	85th Battn.
MacGillivray, A. D.		
MacGillivray, C. V.	Q.M.-Sergeant	228th Battn.
MacInnis, A. A.	Private	First Depot Battn.
MacIntyre, James		
✚Mackay, A. G.	Private	148th Battn.
Mackay, J. W.	Q.M.-Sergeant	40th Battn.
MacKee, J. L.		
MacKenzie, A.		
‡Mackenzie, A. G.	Gunner	33rd C.F.A.
MacKenzie, H. W.	Private	115th Battn.
Mackenzie, J. T.	Gunner	3rd (N.B. Regt., C.F.A.)
MacKenzie, W. K.	Private	193rd Battn.
Mackie, David	Gunner	61st C.F.A.
Mackie, Peter	Private	119th Battn.
‡MacLaurin, I. W.	Private	42nd Battn.
MacLean, C. H.	Private	No. 7 Stationary Hospital
MacLean, W. C.	Private	106th Battn.
Macleod, H. J.	Private	72nd Battn.
MacMaster, M.	W. T. Operator	R.N.C.V.R.
MacMillan, D. H.	Driver	1st Siege Battery
MacMinn, E. G.	Lieutenant	63rd Reinforcement Co.
MacMinn, R. H.	Lieutenant	B.W.I. Regt.
✚MacNaughton, C. G.	Lance-Corporal	168th Battn.
Macpherson, A.	Cadet	R.A.F.
‡MacRae, A. J.	Private	27th Battn.
Magnac, H. J.	Interpreter	
Malcolm, T. R.	Lieutenant	Canadian Engineers
Malcolmson, J. H. K.		

[113]

NAME	RANK	UNIT
MALLOCH, PAUL	Sergeant	109th Battn.
✦MANN, C. F.		
MANN, C. H.	Lance-Corporal	185th Battn.
MANN, J.		
MANN, J. B.	Paymaster-Sergt.	55th Battn.
MANN, J. C.	Private	134th Battn.
MANN, W.	Sergeant	Can. Engineers
MARBLE, C. D.		
MARCH, J. E. R.	Sapper	Royal Can. Engineers
MARTIN, G. H.	Private	Div. Cyclist Corps
MARTIN, H. L.		Paymaster's Office, Regina
MARTIN, J. W.	Private	160th Battn.
MARTIN, L. B.	Signaller	Div. Cyclists
MARTIN, L. W.	Lieutenant	C.A.S.C.
MARWICK, W. H.	Trumpeter	3rd Siege Battery
MASSICOTTE, H. A.	Cadet	R.A.F.
MASSON, L. L.	Gunner	67th C.F.A.
MASSY, C. R.	Lieutenant	B.W.I. Regt.
MATTHEWS, C. F.	Private	85th Battn.
MATTHEWS, W. H.	Gunner	9th Siege Battery
MAUNDERS, W. H.		
MAY, A. D. (M.C.)	Lieutenant	7th Battn.
MAYCOCK, W. G.	Driver	151st Battn.
MELVIN, W. D.	Sergeant	P.P.C.L.I.
‡MENPES, W.	Lieutenant	92nd Battn.
MERCER, G. F.	Private	1st Tank Battn., Canadian Machine Gun Company
‡MERRIAM, S. G.	Corporal	6th C.M.R.
MERRITT, A. P.	Private	145th Battn.
✦MERRITT, F. G.	Lance-Corporal	85th Battn., N.S. Highlanders Machine Gun Section
MERRITT, W. H.	Private	147th Battn.
MESSIER, A. L.	Cadet	Royal Air Force
MILBY, P. M.		
MILLAR, A. C. B.	Private	1st Depot Battn., B.C. Regt.
MILLAR, H.	Gunner	74th C.F.A.
MILLER, H. McR.	Gunner	R.C.H.A.
‡MILLER, M. P.	Private	C.A.M.C.

Regina, Sask.

Vancouver, B.C.

Regina. Sask.

Vancouver, B.C.

NAME	RANK	UNIT
+MILLETT, J. N. L.	Lieutenant	Royal Flying Corps
MILLIGEN, R. C.	Cadet	R.F.C.
MILLS, W. G.	Gunner	70th C.F.A.
MILNE, A. E.	Q.M.-Sergeant	72nd Battn.
MILNE, N. D.	Corporal	147th Battn.
MILNER, C. H.	Private	193rd Battn.
MILNER, K. V.	Private	1st Depot Battn.
‡MINERS, C. C.	Private	91st Battn.
‡MINGEAUD, A. H.	Sergeant	37th Battn.
+MITCHELL, A.		
MITCHELL, G. S.	Sergeant	C.A.M.C.
MITCHELL, W. E.		
MITTON, G. D.	Gunner	9th Overseas Siege Battn.
MOBLO, H. L.		
MOFFAT, J. A.	Private	Canadian Army Service Corps
MOFFITT, F. S.	Cadet	R.A.F.
+MOIR, D. N.	Trooper	2nd C.M.R.
MONEY, C.	Paymaster-Sergt.	168th Battn.
‡MONSON, C. G.	Private	49th Battn.
MONTGOMERY, E. B. W.	Trooper	12th C.M.R.
MONTGOMERY, G. C.	Private	187th Battn.
‡MONTGOMERY, H. B.		
MOORE, A. J.	Cadet	Royal Air Force
+MOORE, C. G. E.	Private	8th Battn.
MOORE, J. R.	Cadet	Royal Air Force
+MOORE, J. W.	Gunner	72nd C.F.A.
MOORE, S. G.	Private	C.A.S.C.
MOORE, W. E.	Gunner	64th C.F.A.
MOORE, W. H.		2nd Depot Battn.
MORAN, F. W.	Gunner	McGill Siege Battery
MORASH, J. R.	Cadet	Royal Air Force
MORELL, A. H.	Gunner	24th C.F.A.
§MORGAN, F. W. L.	Corporal	166th Battn.
MORLAND, J.	Private	C.A.M.C.
MORLEY, G. K.	Private	R.A.M.C.
MORREN, J.	Private	Canadian Engineers
MORRISON, C. F.	Gunner	C.F.A.
+MORRISON, D. S.		

NAME	RANK	UNIT
MORRISON, W. H.	Bombardier	10th Siege Battery
MORRISON, W. McI.	Gunner	9th Siege Battery
MORRISSETTE, J. P. A.	Private	C.O.T.C., Laval
MORROW, J.	Paymaster-Sergt.	40th Battn.
MORROW, M. H.	Signaller	Div. Sig. Corps
✦MORTON, J. M.	Lieutenant	31st Battn.
MORTON, W.	Sergeant	194th Battn.
MOSHER, A. T.		Royal Air Force
MOSHER, W. A.	Cadet	Royal Air Force
MOSS, N. E.	Private	110th Battn.
✦MUIR, D. MacN.	Sergeant	7th Battn.
MULCAHEY, T. J.	Private	No. 9 Stationary Hospital
MULHERN, B. E.	Private	1st Canadian Tank Battn.
MULLETT, C. J.	Cadet	Royal Air Force
MULLIGAN, L. A. A.	Cadet	Royal Air Force
MUNRO, J. J.	Captain	174th Battn.
MURDUFF, A. S.	Private	64th Battery
MURPHY, C. J.	Sapper	Royal Can. Engineers
MURPHY, L. D.	Private	70th Battery
MURRAY, A. D.	Lieutenant	C.F.A.
✦MURRAY, B.	Private	185th Battn.
MURRAY, G. H.	Sergeant	4th Pioneer Battn.
✦MURRAY, N.	Private	Royal Air Force
‡MURRAY, N. W.	Lieutenant	P.P.C.L.I.
MURRELL, E.	Sergeant	1st Div. Headquarters
McALPINE, A. C.	Sapper	Canadian Engineers
McALPINE, A. F.	Gunner	10th Siege Battery
McCALLUM, A. V.	Private	Forestry Battn.
McCALLUM, H. M.	Private	1st Depot Battn.
‡McCALLUM, J. McF.	Lieutenant	Canadian Infantry
McCARTHY, L. M.	Captain	Canadian Infantry
McCARTNEY, W. N.	Gunner	71st Battery
McCLAFFERTY, J. K.	Gunner	C.G.A.
McCLELLAND, C. H.	Driver	68th C.F.A.
McCLELLAND, T. A.	Cadet	68th C.F.A.
McCLENNAN, M. T.	Gunner	R.C.H.A.
McCLUSKEY, H. D.	Gunner	72nd C.F.A.
McCORMICK, G. R.	Corporal	24th Battn.

St. John, N. B.

Charlottetown, P. E. I.

St. John, N. B.

Charlottetown, P. E. I.

NAME	RANK	UNIT
✦McCoy, J. S.	Sergeant	89th Battn.
McCrea, E. A.	Col.-Sergt. . . .	231st Battn.
McCulloch, H. S.	Private	209th Battn.
McCusker, L. J. H.	Lieutenant . . .	107th Battn.
McDonald, A. W.	Cadet	Royal Flying Corps
McDonald, D. G.	Corporal	13th Reserve Battn.
✦McDonald, H. A.	Captain	Highland Cyclists
McDonald, T.	Private	54th Battn.
McDonald, V.	Private	137th Battn.
‡McDonough, C. E.		
‡McDougald, C. G. (m.m.) .	Sergeant	72nd Battn.
McDougall, A. G.	Private	64th C.F.A.
McEown, C. E.		Royal Flying Corps
McEwen, N. D.	Private	69th C.F.A.
McFadyen, W. J.	Cadet	Royal Air Force
McGannon, C. W.	Seaman	R.N.C.V.R.
McGarrity, J. P.	Private	172nd Battn.
McGaw, M. W. M.	Private	C.A.M.C.
McGibbon, A. A.	Air Mechanic. .	Royal Flying Corps
✦McGibbon, W. P.		
McGimpsey, Thos.		
McGinn, W. G. F.	Gunner	70th C.F.A.
McGovern, W. F. (m.c. and bar) . . . . : . . .	Lieutenant . . .	13th C.F.A.
McGregor, D. J.	Private	116th Battn.
McGregor, M.		
McHardy, T. E.	Lieutenant . . .	British West India Regt.
✦McInerney, G. V.	Lieutenant . . .	C.F.A.
McInerney, J. R.	Gunner . . .	6th Can. Siege Battery
McInnes, B.	Lance-Corporal .	Man. Regt. Depot
McIntosh, W. B.	Private	10th Battn.
McIntyre, D. C.	Gunner	2nd Brigade, Canadian Reserve Battn.
McIntyre, J. A.	Private	216th Battn.
McIntyre, J. I.	Cadet Wing . .	Royal Flying Corps
✦McIntyre, L. H.	Cadet	Royal Flying Corps
‡McKay, A. S.	Private	50th Battn.
McKay, J. B.	Lieutenant . . .	132nd Battn.

NAME	RANK	UNIT
McKay, J. R.	Gunner	10th Siege Battery
McKee, D.	Sergeant	119th Battn.
McKenna, E. P.	Cadet	Royal Flying Corps
McKenzie, H.	"A.B." Writer	Paymaster's Staff, H.M.C.S. *Niobe*
McKenzie, K.	Cadet	Royal Flying Corps
McKenzie, L. A.	Gunner	68th C.F.A.
McKenzie, W. H.	Gunner	4th C.F.A.
McKinnon, A. R.	Corporal	168th Battn.
McKnight, D.	Private	100th Battn.
McLachlan, A. O.	Private	C.A.D.C.
McLarren, A. F.	Gunner	14th H.B.A.C.
McLatchy, J. H.	Sergeant	236th Battn.
McLaughlin, J. W.		70th C.F.A.
✠McLea, K. W.		3rd Div. Can. Amm. Col.
McLean, A. R.	Corporal	72nd Battn.
McLean, C. H.	Gunner	2nd Heavy Battery
McLean, E.	Corporal	52nd C.F.A.
McLean, K.	Private	231st Battn.
McLean, M. A.	Cadet	Royal Flying Corps
McLean, W. H.	Private	Royal Flying Corps
McLeod, C. R.	Cadet	R.A.F.
McLeod, H. H. D.	Staff Q.M.S.	40th Battn.
McLeod, J. G.	Private	46th Battn.
McMahon, J. A.	Private	1st Depot Battn.
McMullen, A. R.	Captain	C.A.P.C.
McNabb, J. D.	Private	196th Battn.
McNamara, J. M.	Private	1st Depot Battn.
McNeice, T. G.	Lance-Corporal	16th Battn.
McNeill, H. B.	Gunner	63rd C.F.A.
McNeill, J. D.	Gunner	61st C.F.A.
McPhail, A. V.	Lieutenant	Royal Flying Corps
McPhail, E. W.	Sapper	1st Battn.
McPhail, L. L.	Private	C.A.M.C.
McQuade, W. C.	Lieutenant	104th Battn.
McQuillan, R. A.	Cadet	Royal Flying Corps
McRae, F.	Cadet	R.A.F.
McRobert, J. A. V.	Cadet	Royal Flying Corps

NAME	RANK	UNIT
McTeer, D.	Gunner	61st Battery, C.F.A.
✦McWilliam, J.	Private	32nd Battn.
✦Nairn, W.	Gunner	68th Depot Field Battery, C.F.A.
Nash, R. F.	Gunner	3rd Siege Battery
Nason, C. G.	Sapper	6th Field Co., Can. Engineers
Nellis, R. J.	Driver	64th C.F.A.
✦Nelson, A. B.	Private	46th Battn.
Nelson, E. S.		
Nelson, F. H.	Trooper	8th Mounted Rifles
Nesbitt, F. P.	Private	58th Battn.
Nesbitt, W.	Driver	"C" Battery, R.C.H.A.
Nesbitt, W. A. H.	Gunner	34th C.F.A.
Neville, E. V.	Sergeant	1st Depot Battn., N.S. Regt.
Neville, W. J.	Sergeant	91st Battn.
Newall, P. G.	Private	92nd Battn.
Newart, F. G.		
Newby, H. J.		
✦Nicholls, W. H.	Lieutenant	235th Battn.
Nicholson, R. R. N.	Private	194th Battn.
Nickerson, E. C.	Cadet	Royal Flying Corps
Nickerson, M. H.	Private	6th Can. Field Engineers
Nickle, C.	Cadet	Royal Flying Corps
Nicol, D. A.	Private	175th Battn.
Nicoll, R.		
‡Nicolson, R. A.	Staff-Sergeant	151st Battn.
Nixon, C. B.	Private	168th Battn.
Nixon, M. E.	Gunner	9th Siege Battery
✦Noble, J. A.	Private	P.P.C.L.I.
Noble, W.	Private	20th Battn.
Noonan, J. F.	Private	248th Battn.
Noonan, P. (M.M.)	Sergeant	36th Howitzer Battery
✦Norman, A. L.	Driver	29th Battery, C.F.A.
Nyffeler, F.	Private	F. Company, 3rd Leicester Regt.
Oatman, E. R.	Private	228th Battn.

THE ROYAL BANK OF CANADA

NAME	RANK	UNIT
‡O'Brien, R.	Private	C.A.M.C., 4th Sanitary Sec.
O'Callaghan, A. J.		
Ockenden, E. F.	Lance-Corporal	49th Battn.
O'Connell, J. F.	Private	185th Battn.
O'Donnell, C. G.	Cadet	Royal Air Force
O'Donnell, N. L.		
O'Grady, J. R.	Lieutenant	17th C.F.A.
O'Keefe, T. P.	Gunner	36th C.F.A.
Olive, A. K.	Private	R.N.W.M.P.
O'Neill, K. J.	Private	118th Battn.
‡O'Reilly, P. R.	Lance-Corporal	1st Nfld. Regt.
Ostrander, J. P. B.	Private	194th Battn.
O'Toole, A. G.	Gunner	10th Siege Battery
‡Packer, J.	Private	46th Battn.
Page, E. H.	Private	219th Battn.
Paget, R. J.	Captain	Canadian Infantry
‡Palmer, E. A.		
Pappin, W. McL.	Private	2nd Depot Battn., E.O. Regt.
Park, R.		
Parker, G. A.	Private	168th Battn.
Parker, G. R.	Signaller	9th Siege Battery
Parlmer, E. R.	Private	Can. Record Office
Partridge, H. M.	Private	8th Battn.
Partridge, S. A.		
Paterson, A. E.		
✦Pattison, C. E.	Lieutenant	Aviation Corps, R.N.
✦Pauline, V. R.	Lieutenant	Royal Flying Corps
Peake, H. W.	Lieutenant	No. 5 Siege Battery
Peart, C. D.		
Peers, R. H. C.	Staff-Sergt.	1st Depot Battn., N.S.
✦Pelluet, R.	Private	200th Battn.
Penney, E. W.		Can. Records Office
Pennington, C. M.	Private	Headquarters Staff, Paymaster's Dept., U.S. Navy
Pepin, E. M.		U.S. Navy
Percy, E.	Bugler	148th Battn.
Perrier, R. J. A.	Corporal	227th Battn.

New York Agency, 68 William Street.

New York Agency, 68 William Street.

NAME	RANK	UNIT
PERRIN, J. H.	Gunner	70th C.F.A.
PERRY, L. J.	Corporal	C.A.S.C.
PERRY, R. W.	Private	Motor Cycle Corps
+PETERS, A. W.	Private	72nd Battn.
PETERS, D. G. (M.C.)	Lieutenant	236th Battn.
PETERS, W. H.	Cadet	Royal Air Force
PHILIP, J.	Private	16th Battn.
+PHILLIPS, A.	Private	142nd Battn.
PHILLIPS, A. J.		
‡PHINNEY, C. R.	Gunner	50th C.F.A.
PICKARD, H. J.	Corporal	25th Battn.
+PICKERING, R. B.		
PICKUP, S.	Sergeant	No. 1 Section, 5th D.A.C.
+PIGG, RAYMOND		78th Battn.
PINDER, A. L.	Private	C.M.G. Depot
POIRIER, W. P.	Cadet	Royal Flying Corps
POOLE, V. B.	Gunner	9th Can. Siege Battery
POPE, J. J.		
PORRITT, C. R.	Driver	52nd C.F.A.
PORTER, J. F.	Driver	Divisional Amm. Column
‡PORTER, L.	Private	87th Battn.
PORTER, R.	Lance-Corporal	43rd Battn.
PORTNALL, C. O.		
POTTER, J. L.	Private	37th Battn.
POUDRIER, H. O.	Cadet	Royal Air Force
POW, H. W.	Gunner	R.C.H.A.
POWE, F. W. G.	Private	C.A.M.C.
PRANGLEY, G. W.	Gunner	110th Battn.
PREVOST, S. A.	Private	35th Battn.
PRICE, E.		Royal Canadian Navy
PRICE, J. H. W.	Lance-Corporal	28th Battn.
PRIDHAM, W. C.		
PRIEUR, J. A.		R.C.H.A.
PRINCE, W. S.	Sapper	Div. Sig. Corps
+PRINGLE, W. R.	Private	C.A.M.C.
PRIZEMAN, W. H.		
PULFER, L. J.		
PUMPHREY, E. J.	Private	1st Depot Battn.

NAME	RANK	UNIT
PURDY, W. J.	Private	1st Depot Battn.
PUTNAM, A. R.		
‡PUTNAM, J. M.	Private	82nd Battn.
QUICK, L-H. ST. P.	Gunner	Royal Field Artillery
QUINN, A. L.	Private	1st Depot Battn., W.O.R.
*RACEY, B. R.	Private	14th Battn.
RADFORD, A. F. (M.M.)	Sergeant	50th Battn.
RAE, W.	Gunner	79th C.F.A.
RAFUSE, S. A.	Sergeant	106th Battn.
RAILTON, R. R.		
✦RALSTON, J. A.	Signaller	3rd Battn.
RAMSAY, F. M.	Lieutenant	R.N.A.S.
RANKIN, E. B.		Royal Nfld. Regt.
RAWLINS, J. M.	Private	Royal Newfoundland Regt.
READ, A. F.	Gunner	74th Battery, C.F.A.
READ, T. D.	Sapper	Divisional Signallers
REESOR, W. C.	Private	7th Battn.
REIBER, C. E.	Corporal	1st Depot Battn., Calgary
REID, A.	Private	8th Battn.
REID, E. J.	Private	C.A.M.C.
REID, G. E.		C.A.M.C.
REID, J. S.	Private	24th Battn.
REID, M. C.		
RELYEA, R. E.	Driver	51st Howitzer Battery
RENTON, A. W.	Bugler	11th Battn.
REYNOLDS, R. H.	Cadet	Royal Air Force.
RHIND, C. E.	Private	219th Battn.
RHODY, B. P.	Cadet	Royal Air Force
RICE, W.	Private	184th Battn.
RICHARDS, S.	Private	30th Battn,
✦RICHARDSON, J. M.	Corporal	66th Battn.
RICHARDSON, L. M.	Captain	54th Battn.
RICHARDSON, R. P.	Corporal	Can. Tel. Corps
✦RICHES, J. H.	Private	33rd Battn.
RICHMOND, J. F.	Private	158th Battn.
RIDDELL, W. R.	Lieutenant	C.A.P.C.

NAME	RANK	UNIT
RIEGER, R. A.	Corporal	C.G.R.
RIGGS, E. S.	Private	Canadian Engineers
‡RIPLEY L. W.	Private	193rd Battn.
RISSER, W. A.	Gunner	Depot, R.C.H.A.
ROBB, M. J.	Lieutenant	4th C.M.R.
ROBERTS, E.	Cadet	Royal Flying Corps
ROBERTS, T. K.	-.	No.10 Forestry and Railway Construction Co.
ROBERTSON, D. W.	Gunner	72nd Queen's Battery
‡ROBERTSON, S.	Captain	1st Newfoundland Regt.
ROBINSON, B. H. P.		
ROBINSON, F. G.	Private	78th C.F.A.
ROBINSON, G. S.	Signaller	Siege Artillery
ROBINSON, H. D.	Private	196th Battn.
ROBINSON, J.	Private	202nd Battn.
ROBINSON, J. H.	Sergeant	85th Battn.
ROBINSON, W. G.	Gunner	70th C.F.A.
ROCHE, G. E.		
RODGERS, J. H. M.	Private	York and Simcoe Foresters
‡RODWELL, H. J.	Private	183rd Battn.
ROE, G. M. C.	Staff-Sergt.	C.A.P.C.
ROE, S. F. D.	Lieutenant	R.A.F.
ROEBER, W. J. D.	Private	25th U.S. Cavalry
ROENIGK, F. W.	Gunner	67th C.F.A.
ROGERS, T. B.	Lieutenant	
ROMERO, D.	Sergeant	Sanitary Corps, Porto Rico Regt.
RORISON, B. T.		
ROSS, C. S.	Gunner	5th Siege Battery
ROSS, J. K.	Cadet	Royal Air Force
ROSS, K.	Trooper	Royal Canadian Dragoons
ROSS, R.		
ROSS, R. A.	Gunner	63rd C.F.A.
ROSS, W. F.	Lance-Corporal	10th Battn.
+ROSS, W. P.	Private	196th Western University Battn.
ROTHWELL, G. H.		
ROVIRA, A. G.	Private	373rd Infantry, U.S.A.

NAME	RANK	UNIT
ROWLAND, J. A.	Gunner	72nd C.F.A.
‡ROWLANDS, A.	Gunner	4th Div. Amm. Column
ROY, L. P. J.	Cadet	Royal Flying Corps
RUDOLPH, S. C.	Private	Divisional Signal Corps
RUGGLES, W. C.	Pay Sergeant	1st Depot Battn., N.S.
RUMBALL, F. H.	Gunner	63rd C.F.A.
RUSHTON, F. W. (M.C.)	2nd Lieutenant	3rd Battn.
RUSS, J. P.	Corporal	65th Battn.
RUSSELL, H.	Wheeler	1st Div. Amm. Column
RUSSELL, J. B.	Sapper	Canadian Engineers
RUSSELL, R. C.	Lance-Corporal	1st Depot Battn., B.C. Regt.
RUTHERFORD, J. S.	Private	24th Battn.
RUTTAN, V. H.	Driver	C.A.S.C.
RYAN, A. M.	Private	4th Battn.
+SALUSBURY, N. H. P.	Driver	C.A.S.C.
SANDERSON, E. R.	Private	156th Battn.
SANDERSON, J. D.	Cadet	Royal Air Force
SANDILANDS, W. T.		
*SAUNDERS, J. T.	Trooper	6th C.M.R.
SCHAEFER, F. W.	Gunner	1st Canadian Heavy Battery, C.G.A.
SCHARFE, J. A.	Gunner	74th Battery, C.F.A.
SCHJOLSETH, C.		Royal Air Force
SCOTT, C. L.	Private	First Depot Battn., B.C.
+SCOTT, S. W.	Lance-Corporal	129th Battn.
SCOUGALL, J. M.	Qmr.-Sergeant	124th Battn.
SCRIVEN, J. A.	Gunner	10th Halifax Siege Battery
SCRIVENER, H. L.		
SEABORN, J. McK.		
SEAR, H. L.	Gunner	9th Siege Battery
SEATH, G.	Gunner	77th C.F.A.
SELKIRK, M. L.	2nd Lieutenant	Royal Air Force
+SELLERS, S. G.		
‡SEVERS, W. E.	Gunner	9th C.F.A.
‡SHANNON, W. A.	Paymaster-Sergt.	55th Battn.
+SHARP, F. H.		
SHARP, W. J.	Corporal	66th C.F.A.

Winston Hotel

	RANK	UNIT
...NO, J. A.	Gunner	72nd C.F.A.
R... DS, A.	Gunner	4th Div. Amm. Column
...L. P. J.	Cadet	Royal Flying Corps
...PH, S. C.	Private	Divisional Signal Corps
...KLES, W. C.	Pay Sergeant	1st Depot Battn., N.S.
...MBALL, F. H.	Gunner	63rd C.F.A.
RUSHTON, F. W. (M.C.)	2nd Lieutenant	3rd Battn.
RUSS, J P.	Corporal	65th Battn.
RUSSELL, H.	Wheeler	1st Div. Amm. Column
RUSSELL, J. B.	Sapper	Canadian Engineers
RUSSELL, R. C.	Lance-Corporal	1st Depot Battn., B.C. Regt.
...RUTHERFORD, J S	Private	24th Battn.
RUTTAN Y. H	Driver	C.A.S.C.
RYAN A. M	Private	4th Battn.
◆SAINSBURY, N H P.	Driver	C.A.S.C.
SANDERSON, E. R	Private	156th Battn.
SANDERSON, J. D.	Cadet	Royal Air Force
SANDILANDS, W. T.		
◆SAUNDERS, J. T.	Trooper	6th C.M.R.
SCHAEFER, F W.	Gunner	1st Canadian Heavy Battery, C.G.A.
SCHARFE, J. A.	Gunner	74th Battery, C.F.A.
SCHJOLSETH, C.		Royal Air Force
SCOTT, C. L.	Private	First Depot Battn., B.C.
◆SCOTT, S. W.	Lance-Corporal	129th Battn.
SCOUGALL, J. M.	Qmr.-Sergeant	124th Battn.
SCRIVEN, J. A.	Gunner	10th Halifax Siege Battery
SCRIVENER, H. L.		
SEABORN, J. McK.		
SEAR, H. L.	Gunner	9th Siege Battery
SEATH, G.	Gunner	77th C.F.A.
SELKIRK, M. L.	2nd Lieutenant	Royal Air Force
◆SELLEFT S. G.		
‡SEVERS W. E.	Gunner	9th C.F.A.
‡SHANNON W A.	Paymaster-Sergt.	55th Battn.
◆SHAW T H.		
SHAW J	Corporal	66th C.F.A.

Havana, Cuba.

NAME	RANK	UNIT
✦Sharpe, H. V.	Gunner	34th C.F.A.
Shaw, H. J.	Gunner	10th Siege Battery
Shaw, J. C.	Gunner	2nd Heavy Artillery
‡Shaw, R.	Lieutenant	R.A.F.
✦Shearer, T. P.	Private	3rd Div. Train, C.A.S.C.
Sheldon, J. S.	Private	186th Battn.
Shepherd, T. R.	Private	C.A.M.C.
Shepherd, W. E.	Gunner	Royal Can. Horse Artillery
Sheppard, C. M.	Private	24th Battn.
Sherman, F. J.	Captain	C.A.P.C.
✦Sherman, L. S.	Lance-Corporal	Royal Sussex Regt.
Sheriffs, W. R.	Cadet	Royal Air Force
✦Shields, D. DeV.	Private	112th Battn.
Shields, S. B.		
Shimmen, J. H.	Private	C.A.S.C.
✦Shore, J. A. M.	Lieutenant	186th Battn.
Shorey, S. O.	Gunner	27th C.F.A.
Simon, P. M.	2nd Class Seaman	2-C-1 Battn., U.S. Navy
Simpson, C. B.	Corporal	Canadian Engineers
Simpson, H. G.	Gunner	34th C.F.A.
Simpson, R. T.	Gunner	67th C.F.A.
Simpson, R. T. H.	Private	31st Battn.
Simpson, W. J.	Private	170th Battn.
‡Sims, V.	Private	78th Battn.
‡Singleton, A.	Private	2nd Battn.
✦Skeaff, J. M.	Lieutenant	92nd Battn.
Skene, O. E.	Private	66th Battn.
Sly, A. F.		
Small, H. J.	Gunner	33rd C.F.A.
Smith, A.		
Smith, A. F.		
Smith, A. G. H.	Private	C.A.P.C.
Smith, A. R.	Paymaster-Sergt.	112th Battn.
Smith, C. K.	Lieutenant	4th Con. B.W.I. Regt.
‡Smith, F. C.	Sergeant	131st Battn.
Smith, G. J.	Sergeant	10th Siege Battery
Smith, H. H.	Private	No. 3 General Hospital
✦Smith, J. T.	Private	8th Battn.

NAME	RANK	UNIT
SMITH, P. J.	Paymaster-Sergt.	2nd Quebec Regt.
SMITH, R.	Lieutenant	11th Battn.
✠SMITH, R. H.	Private	C.A.M.C.
‡SMITH, S. W.	Corporal	P.P.C.L.I.
✠SMITH, T. V. G.	Sapper	Canadian Engineers
SMITH, W. P.		
SMITH, W. R.	Private	174th Battn.
✠SMYTH, F. A.	Private	162nd Battn.
SMYTH, R. S. V.	Private	Royal Flying Corps
SNELGROVE, E. G.		
SNELL, L. L.	Private	No. 1 Forestry Battn.
✠SNOW, F. W.	Lance-Corporal	1st Newfoundland Regt.
✠SNOWDON, J. L.	Private	160th Battn.
SNOWDON, M. J.	Driver	3rd Section Divisional Amm. Column
SOANES, E.	Gunner	67th C.F.A.
‡SPENCE, C. M. V. (M.M.)	Lieutenant	21st Battn.
✠SPENCE, R. E.	Sergt.-Major	6th C.F.A.
SPERO, W. P.	Captain	135th Battn.
SQUIRE, A. G.	Lieutenant	1st Battn. West India Regt.
SQUIRE, T. E.	Cadet	Royal Air Force
SQUIRES, R. H.	Cadet	R.A.F.
‡STABLEFORD, F.	Private	46th Battn.
‡STAFFORD, J. H.	Private	16th Battn.
STANLEY, F. A.	Bombardier	36th Howitzer Battery
STARK, R.	Private	139th Battn.
STARKE, A. M.	Private	1st Reinforcing Co., 5th R.H.C.
STATHAM, E. H.	Private	48th Battn.
STEEDMAN, A. W.	Cadet	Royal Air Force
‡STEELE, C. F.	Private	153rd Battn.
✠STEELE, J. H.	Private	P.P.C.L.I.
✠STEIN, C. D. P.	Sapper	Canadian Engineers
✠STEPHEN, C. N.		
‡STEPHEN, H. J.	Private	5th Battn.
STEPHEN, W. M.	Private	B. C. Cycle Platoon
STEPHENS, A. E.	Private	85th Battn.
STEPHENS, F. L.	Private	157th Battn.

London, England, Princes St. E.

Rio de Janeiro, Brazil

London , England , Princes St. E.C.

Rio de Janeiro, Brazil

NAME	RANK	UNIT
Stephens, J. D.		177th Battn.
Stephens, R. M.		
Sterns, H. E.		
Stevens, E. V.		
‡Stevens, F. H.	Sergeant	7th Battn.
Stewart, D. J.	Gunner	10th Siege Battery
Stewart, E. W. H.	Lieutenant	23rd Battn.
Stewart, H. L.	Private	69th C.F.A.
Stewart, J.	Private	63rd Battn.
Stewart, J. McL.	Cadet	Royal Air Force
‡*Stewart, T.	Sergeant-Major	8th Battn.
Stewart, W. C.	Private	C.A.S.C.
Stinson, J. E.	Cadet	R.A.F.
*Stone, B. C.	Private	P.P.C.L.I.
Stone, J. G.		89th Battn.
Stoneman, H. K.	Sergeant	Forestry Battn.
Strachan, A.	Private	C.A.S.C.
Strachan, W. S.	Private	4th Div. Train
‡Strong, H. P.	Sergeant	145th Battn.
Strople, H. G. A.	Private	64th Battn.
Stuart, A.	Corporal	Royal Fusiliers
Stubbs, H. C.	Private	Royal Flying Corps
Summerhayes, R. C.	Lance-Corporal	Special Service
Sutherby, R. E.	Driver	53rd C.F.A.
Sutherland, H. B.	Gunner	67th C.F.A.
Sutherland, R. M.	Gunner	10th Siege Battery
Sydenham, O. S.	Sergeant	10th Battn.
Tache, J. G. C.	Private	C.O.T.C.
Taitt, N. R.	Lieutenant	
Tanner, B. H.	Paymaster-Sergt.	130th Battn.
Tanner, H. R. (m.c.)	Lieutenant	24th Battn.
Tassie, J. S. G.	Lieutenant	R. F. Artillery
Tate, J. R.	Gunner	68th C.F.A.
Taylor, P. B.	Major and Brevet Lt.-Col.	77th Battn.
Taylor, R. A.	Private	51st Battn.
Taylor, W. T.	Private	13th Battn.

NAME	RANK	UNIT
TEASDALE, C. A..	Cadet	Royal Air Force
TEEPLE, J. H..	Gunner	63rd C.F.A.
TEEVAN, T. F..	Private	67th Battn.
TELFER, H. C..	Lieutenant . . .	Royal Flying Corps
+TEMPLE, C. C..		
TESSIER, R. McN.	Lance-Corporal .	1st Newfoundland Regt.
THIBAULT, A. H..	Private	227th Battn.
+THOMPSON, C. G.	Lieutenant . . .	Can. Field Artillery
THOMPSON, C. S..	Private	P.P.C.L.I.
THOMPSON, F. A..	Gunner	9th Siege Battery
THOMPSON, G. P.	Private	102nd Battalion
THOMPSON, J. F..	Paymaster-Sergt.	232nd Battn.
THOMSON, FREDERICK . . .	Private	43rd Battn.
THOMSON, H. J..	Private	151st Battn.
THOMSON, J.	Gunner	67th C.F.A.
THOMSON, W. P..	Private	7th Battn.
THORNTON, N. H.	Private	49th Battn.
THORP, C. A..	Signalman . . .	R.C.N.V.R.
+THORSTEINSON, F..	Private	10th Battn.
THURSTONS, H. S. Y. . . .	Gunner	34th C.F.A.
+TILLEY, H. S. T.	Private	1st Depot Battn., 1st Central Ontario Regt.
TINDALE, A. S.	Gunner	3rd Can. Division Artillery
TINDALL, O. L.	Gunner . . .	R.C.H.A.
TODD, C. C.	Private	187th Machine Gun Corps
TODD, HENRY		
TOMPKINS, N. C.	Private	26th Battn.
TOOTHILL, W. A.	Leading Seaman	Royal Naval Reserve
TORRADO, E.	Private	Medical Corps, Base Hospital, San Juan
+TOWER, R. E..	Corporal	6th C.M.R.
TRAVERS, R. G. H.	Captain	20th Battn.
TREPANIER, W. P..	Gunner	74th C.F.A.
TRIGO, J..		
‡TROY, L. T..	Flight Lieut. . .	R.A.F.
TRUNKFIELD, V. J.	2nd Clerk . . .	Royal Air Force
+TUACH, D. M..	Private	Royal Fusiliers
TUCK, D. C.	Gunner	Siege Artillery

NAME	RANK	UNIT
TULLY, N. J.	Private	127th Battn.
+TUPPER, M. L.	Captain	112th Battn.
+TURNBULL, G. A.	Sergeant	40th Battn.
TURNBULL, G. V.	Gunner	9th Siege Battery
TURNBULL, J.	Gunner	74th C.F.A.
+TURNBULL, W. J. (M.C.)	Acting Captain	Can. Field Artillery
TURNER, A. V.	Gunner	C.F.A.
TURNER, J. B.	Sergeant	65th Battn.
TURNER, S. A.		8th Can. Inf. Brig. Signallers
*TUTT, F. H.	Private	14th Battn.
TYLER, G.	Private	1st Depot Battn., Sask.
TYNER, H. R.	Captain	3rd Battn. Dorset Regt.
TYSON, G.	Private	23rd Battn.
UNDERHILL, R.	Sergeant	Territorial Forces
UNDERWOOD, T. H.	Private	63rd Battn.
UREN, A. C.	Asst. Paymaster	Royal Naval Reserve
VALDEZATE, I.		
VALE, G. ST. J., JR.	Trooper	20th C.M.R.
‡VAN ALLEN, W. H.	Lance-Corporal	29th Light Horse of Sask.
+VAN KLEEK, G. W.	Private	209th Battn.
VAN WYCK, T. H.	Cadet	Royal Flying Corps
VANN, A. J.	Captain	
VICKERS, E. I.		
VICKERSON, J. L.	Gunner	78th C.F.A.
VOADEN, C. E.	Private	C.A.M.C.
+VOELKER, C. R.	Lieutenant	192nd Battn.
VYSE, E. T.	Lieutenant	12th Battn.
WAKELIN, E. V.		Siberian Exp. Force
WALDIE, W.	Corporal	62nd Battn.
+WALLACE, C. W.	Private	231st Battn.
‡WALLACE, F. C.	Lieutenant	
+WALLACE, H.	Private	17th Battn.
WALLACE, R. A. (M.C.)	Lieutenant	168th Siege Battery, R.G.A.
WALLER, G. DEW.	Gunner	74th C.F.A.
+WALLIS, I. N.	Trooper	C.M.R.

NAME	RANK	UNIT
WALTER, M. M.	Private	C.A.M.C.
WARD, S. W.	Gunner	72nd C.F.A.
§WARNER, F. M.	Lieutenant	4th Royal Scots
WATSON, G. R. D.	Lieutenant	R.N.V.R.
WATT, D. J.	Sergeant	55th C.F.A.
WATT, R. A. McR.	Private	R.A.M.C.
WEAVER, H. C.	Private	7th Battn.
WEAVER, W. C.	Paymaster-Sergt.	154th Battn.
WEBSTER, G. L.	Cadet	Royal Flying Corps
WEBSTER, W. J.	Private	Paymaster's Staff
WEEKS, T. B.	Lance-Corporal	73rd Battn.
WEIR, J. J.	Gunner	67th C.F.A.
WEIR, T.	Corporal	11th C.M.R.
‡*WELLS, D. P.	Private	13th Battn.
✦WELLS, G. E.		
WELLWOOD, W. G.	Gunner	68th C.F.A.
WENSLEY, J. H.		
✦WEST, C. F.	Private	C.A.P.C.
WEST, W. H. L.	Sapper	6th Field Co., Can. Engineers
WESTBROOK, L. A.	Cadet	Royal Flying Corps
WETMORE, L. C.	Gunner	9th Siege Battery
WHATMORE, K.		
WHIDDEN, E. L.	Gunner	10th Siege Battery
WHITE, F. J.	Gunner	McGill Siege Battery
‡WHITE, G.	Gunner	10th Halifax Siege Battery
WHITE, J.	Private	228th Battn.
✦WHITE, R. B.	Sergeant	1st Newfoundland Regt.
WHITEHEAD, F. W. F.	Lieutenant	Royal Highlanders of Canada
WHITEHEAD, G. V.	Lieutenant	148th Battn.
WICKETT, R. A. W.	Private	49th Battn.
WICKS, W. E.	Private	Div. Cycle Corps
‡WICKWIRE, L. H.	Private	193rd Battn.
WIDMEYER, L. H.	Private	248th Battn.
WILKINS, A. H. J.	Corporal	79th C.F.A.
WILKINSON, A.	Private	43rd Battn.
WILKINSON, W. L.	Gunner	16th C.F.A.
WILLDEY, J. R.		
WILLEY, J. E.		

Port of Spain, Trinidad

Kingston, Jamaica

NAME	RANK	UNIT
✠Williams, A. J.	Private	65th Battn.
Williams, L. A.	Sapper	11th Field Co., C.E.
Williams, W.	Cadet	Royal Air Force
Williams, W. H.	Cadet	Royal Flying Corps
Williamson, E. L.	Private	Sask. Rly. Cons. Co.
✠Williamson, J. C.	Private	176th Battn.
Willis, G. A.	Gunner	47th C.F.A.
Wilmot, A. J.	Private	C.A.M.C.
Wilson, A. B.	Private	147th Battn.
Wilson, G. C.	Private	C.A.M.C.
✠Wilson, G. T.	Corporal	P.P.C.L.I.
Wilson, H. J.	Private	Mechanical Transport, C.A.S.C.
Wilson, J. L.	Private	85th Battn.
Wilson, J. M.	Private	C.A.S.C.
Wilson, R. M.	Gunner	63rd Battery
Wilson, S. N.	Cadet	Royal Flying Corps
Wilson, W.		
Wilson, W. A.	Private	First Tank Battn.
Wilson, W. McL.	Lieutenant	25th Battn.
Wilson, W. P. McK.	Sergeant	1st C.D.A.C.
Winstone, F. J.	Private	C.A.M.C.
Winters, G. W.	Private	219th Battn.
✠Wishart, R. J.	Private	231st Battn.
Withrow, C. A.	Lance-Corporal	85th Battn.
Witter, D. L.	Gunner	54th C.F.A.
✠Wolfe, E. M.	Gunner	67th C.F.A.
‡Wolley-Dod, W. R.		
Womersley, W.	Corporal	184th Battn.
. Wood, A. H.	Cadet	Royal Air Force
Wood, C. R.	Private	18th Battn.
Wood, M. M.	Private	4th Battn.
‡Woodcock, C. E. S.	Lance-Corporal	C.A.S.C.
‡Wright, F.	Private	16th Battn.
✠Wyatt, C. G.	Private	No. 3 General Hospital
Wynn, A. R.	Lieutenant	44th Battn.
Yates, G. G.	Private	196th Battn.
Yool, J.		

NAME	RANK	UNIT
YOUNG, A. S.		
YOUNG, H. A.	Signaller	160th Battn.
YOUNG, L. LeR.	Carpenter . . .	Engineers Corps, Forestry and Railway Con. Depot
YOUNGS, H.	Gunner	63rd C.F.A.
*ZAPFE, A. K.	Corporal . . .	P.P.C.L.I.
ZINCK, A. M.	Private	1st Depot Batt., N.S.
ZINCK, H. A.	Cadet	Royal Flying Corps
ZOLLER, J. I.	Driver	3rd Div. Amm. Column

Bridgetown, Barbados.

...assau, Bahamas.

32-33 VICTORIA

CHAPTER 59

AN ACT TO INCORPORATE THE MERCHANTS BANK OF HALIFAX

[Assented to 22nd June, 1869]

WHEREAS the Honorable Edward Kenny, William Cunard, *Preamble* Thomas C. Kinnear, James Merkill, John Tobin, Thomas E. Kenny, Jeremiah Northup and James B. Duffus, have by their petition prayed that they might be incorporated for the purpose of establishing a bank in the city of Halifax, in the Province of Nova Scotia, and whereas it is desirable to grant the prayer of their petition: Therefore, Her Majesty by and with the advice and consent of the Senate and House of Commons of Canada, enacts as follows:

1. The several persons hereinbefore named and such other per- *Certain per-* sons as shall become shareholders in the corporation to be by this *sons incorpor-* Act created and their assigns, shall be and they are hereby consti- *ated* tuted and declared to be a corporation body corporate and politic by the name of the "Merchants Bank of Halifax," and shall have *Corporate* power to acquire and hold real and immovable estate for the *name and* management of their business not exceeding in annual value five *real estate* thousand dollars, and may sell, alienate or exchange the same and acquire other instead.

2. The business of the Corporation shall be under the manage- *Board of* ment of a President and not more than eight directors, and such *Directors* other officers as may be found necessary.

[147]

Capital Stock, and when to be paid up 3. The capital stock of the Bank hereby incorporated shall be one million of dollars, divided into ten thousand shares of one hundred dollars each, and two hundred thousand dollars of the said stock shall be subscribed for and paid up before the first day of November next, and a further sum of one hundred thousand dollars of the said stock shall be subscribed for and paid up at such time not later than the first day of November, one thousand eight hundred and seventy, as the directors shall appoint, and the remainder thereof, at such time or times as shall be prescribed by future legislation in that behalf, but no instalment shall in any case be called in unless thirty days' previous notice shall have first been given, in two at least of the newspapers published in Halifax, of the time and place appointed for the payment of instalments.

[*Here follow 33 other sections relative to the organization, etc., of the bank.*]

63-64 VICTORIA

CHAPTER 103

AN ACT RESPECTING THE MERCHANTS BANK OF HALIFAX, AND
TO CHANGE ITS NAME TO "THE ROYAL BANK OF CANADA"

[Assented to 14th June, 1900]

WHEREAS the Merchants Bank of Halifax has, by its petition, *Preamble* prayed that it be enacted as hereinafter set forth, and it is expedient to grant the prayer of the said petition: Therefore Her Majesty, by and with the advice and consent of the Senate and House of Commons of Canada, enacts as follows:

1. The name of the Merchants Bank of Halifax is changed *Name* to "The Royal Bank of Canada," but such change in name shall *changed* not in any way impair, alter or affect the rights or liabilities of *Existing* the said Bank, nor in anywise affect any suit or proceeding now *rights preserved* pending, or judgment existing either by or in favour of or against the said Bank, which, notwithstanding such change in name, may be prosecuted, continued, completed and enforced as if this Act had not been passed.

2. Before this Act shall take effect, a general meeting of the *When Act* shareholders of the said Bank shall be called for the purpose of *to come into force* considering it, and a resolution accepting and approving thereof shall be passed by the shareholders present or represented by proxy at such meeting, and a certified copy of such resolution shall, within fifteen days after the passing thereof, be published in *The Canada Gazette*, and this Act shall take effect from the date of such publication.

[149]

63-64 VICTORIA

CHAPTER 104

AN ACT TO AMEND THE "ACT RESPECTING THE MERCHANTS BANK
OF HALIFAX, AND TO CHANGE ITS NAME TO
THE ROYAL BANK OF CANADA"

[Assented to 7th July, 1900]

H ER Majesty, by and with the advice and consent of the Senate and House of Commons of Canada, enacts as follows:—

1900, c. 103, s. 2 repealed 1. Section 2 of the Act of the present session intituled *An Act respecting the Merchants Bank of Halifax, and to change its name to the Royal Bank of Canada* is repealed, and the following section is substituted therefor:—

When Act to come into force "2. The first section of this Act shall come into force upon its publication in *The Canada Gazette*, and the Secretary of State of Canada shall cause it to be so published upon receiving a certificate under the hand of the president of the said bank and the seal of the said bank certifying that the said Act has been approved by a vote of the directors, and upon receiving a sum sufficient to pay the cost of such publication."

Santo Domingo, Dominican Republic

San Juan, Porto Rico

6 EDWARD VII

CHAPTER 157

AN ACT RESPECTING THE ROYAL BANK OF CANADA

[Assented to 13th July, 1906]

WHEREAS the Royal Bank of Canada has by its petition *Preamble* prayed that it be enacted as hereinafter set forth, and it is expedient to grant the prayer of the said petition: Therefore His *1869, c. 59; 187* Majesty, by and with the advice and consent of the Senate and *c. 43; 1900,* House of Commons of Canada, enacts as follows:— *cc. 103, 104*

1. The chief office of the Royal Bank of Canada is hereby *Place of* changed from the City of Halifax, in the Province of Nova Scotia, *chief office* to the City of Montreal, in the Province of Quebec. *changed*

2. The provisions of chapter 59 of the statutes of 1869, intituled *Acts* An Act to incorporate the Merchants Bank of Halifax, and any *amended* amendments of the said Act, in so far as they are inconsistent with this Act, are hereby repealed.

3. This Act shall not take effect unless and until it has been *When Act to* submitted to a general or special meeting of the shareholders of *come into* the said bank and is approved of by a majority of the votes of *force* the shareholders present or represented by proxy at such meeting and entitled to vote thereat, and provided that notice of such meeting and of the proposed change of head office was duly given; and thereupon the foregoing sections of this Act shall come into force upon the publication thereof in the *Canada Gazette*, and the Secretary of State of Canada shall cause them to be so published upon receiving a certificate under the hand of the president and the seal

of the Royal Bank of Canada, certifying that the directors of the said bank have resolved that it is in the interests of the said bank that the chief office should be changed from Halifax to Montreal, and upon receiving a sum sufficient to pay the costs of such publication.

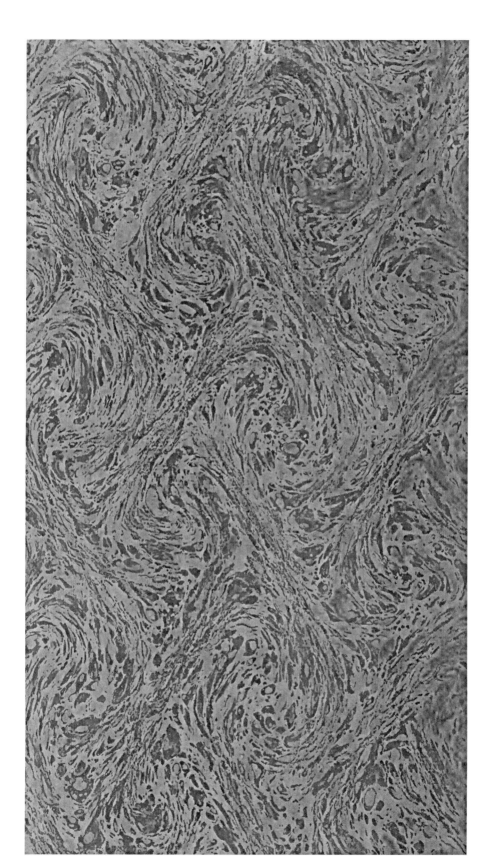

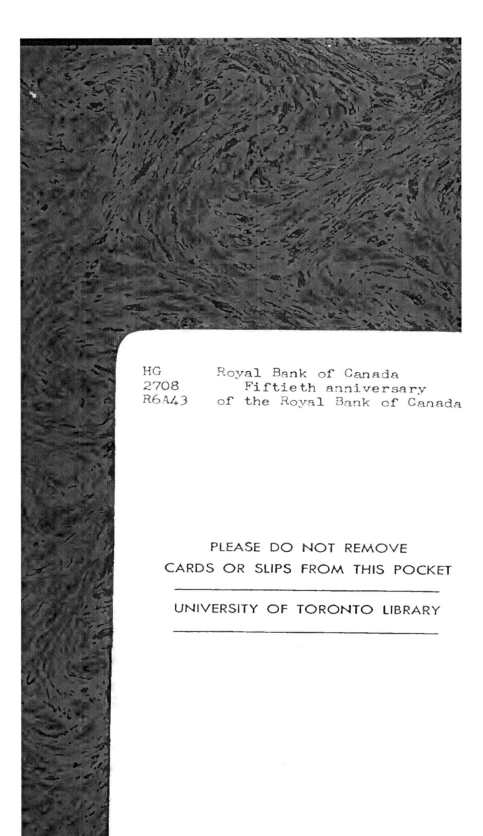

CPSIA information can be obtained at www.ICGtesting.com
Printed in the USA
LVOW101220211012

303777LV00004B/25/P